BRITISH ASSOCIATION OF SPORT AND MEDICINE

MEDICAL ASPECTS OF
BOXING

ORGANIZING COMMITTEE

R. D. JAMES, Dip. P.E. Organizing Secretary
A. L. BASS, M.B., M.R.C.P., D.Phys. Med.
J. L. BLONSTEIN, M.R.C.S., L.R.C.P., D.I.H.
J. G. P. WILLIAMS, M.B., F.R.C.S.Ed., Assistant Secretary, B.A.S.M.

BRITISH ASSOCIATION OF SPORT AND MEDICINE

MEDICAL ASPECTS OF
BOXING

Proceedings of a Conference held at the Goldsmiths' College
London, November, 1963

Edited by

A. L. Bass, J. L. Blonstein
R. D. James, J. G. P. Williams

23893

SYMPOSIUM PUBLICATIONS DIVISION

PERGAMON PRESS

OXFORD · LONDON · EDINBURGH · NEW YORK
PARIS · FRANKFURT

Pergamon Press Ltd., Headington Hill Hall, Oxford
4 & 5 Fitzroy Square, London W.1

Pergamon Press (Scotland) Ltd., 2 & 3 Teviot Place, Edinburgh 1

Pergamon Press Inc., 122 East 55th St., New York 22, N.Y.

Pergamon Press GmbH, Kaiserstrasse 75, Frankfurt-am-Main

First edition 1965

Library of Congress Catalog Card No. 65-18419

Printed in Great Britain by Cheltenham Press Ltd.,
Cheltenham and London

INTRODUCTION

IN VIEW of the increasing volume of publications in both the medical and lay press of articles and comments relating to the medical aspects of boxing, and the amount of emotional furore that appeared to lie behind so many of them, the British Association of Sport and Medicine decided to hold a two-day symposium devoted to all the main aspects of the subject.

Speakers were chosen from among the ranks of eminent medical authorities who were known to be interested, and invitations to the symposium were extended to all official bodies in the medical and sporting worlds, and to the press.

The objects of the symposium were to present in as balanced a way as possible the views of the recognized authorities, and to provide an opportunity for general discussion and debate among all those interested. Since the whole question of the medical aspects of boxing was at that time subject to an inquiry by the Royal College of Physicians, it was decided from the outset that no attempt would be made to reach any corporate conclusion, neither would any recommendations be made. Thus the conference remained simply a forum for public discussion and debate.

Notwithstanding the deliberate intention of the organizers to avoid any suggestion of prejudging the issues prior to the publication of the findings of the Royal College's Commission, inevitably there were apparent certain strong currents of opinion, and it has therefore seemed reasonable, in the light of what was said at the conference, to summarize what was and what was not achieved, and at least to indicate the directions in which the main currents of opinion were flowing.

The epilogue to this collection of papers, dissertations and discussions consists therefore of the Editors' assessment of the conference as a whole. It represents the opinions and reactions of the Editors alone and in no way is to be taken as a statement of the views either of the British Association of Sport and Medicine or of the participants in the conference. Nevertheless, it is hoped that it will stand as an objective appraisal of what was a stimulating and controversial two-day discussion.

CONTENTS

SESSION I

EYE INJURIES

Chairman

SIR ARTHUR PORRITT, Bt., K.C.M.G., K.C.V.O., C.B.E., F.R.C.S.

Chairman, British Association of Sport and Medicine

1

J. H. Doggart, M.D., F.R.C.S.

Consultant Surgeon, Moorfields, Westminster and Central Eye Hospitals
Ophthalmic Surgeon, the Hospital for Sick Children

At a critical stage in the battle of Copenhagen, Nelson heard that his superior officer was signalling him to withdraw. Nelson, who had lost the sight of one eye in an earlier battle, put up a telescope to his blind eye, and quietly remarked that he saw no such signal. This device of facultative Nelsonism, if we can agree to call it so, has proved a godsend for many a clinician seeking to establish the value of a certain treatment, or to research workers bent upon indicting one particular factor as the main cause of a disease. Equipped with facultative Nelsonism they can suppress, belittle or ignore all data which do not advance their thesis.

Some of the medical men dedicated to boxing seem to carry this facultative Nelsonism to the verge of ostrichism. They blandly maintain that injuries sustained in the ring are rare, trivial and transient. They enlarge upon the medical precautions taken, especially at amateur fights, and they go on to recite the toll of damage sustained by players of ball-games. A flying ping-pong ball perhaps scratches a player's cornea. "Ah," say the boxing enthusiasts, wagging their heads in mock solemnity, "he should have stuck to a safe sport like ours."

Let us remember, however, that many of the people whose eyes or brains were badly injured at boxing took warning and left the ring before it was too late. They are soon forgotten by the boxing devotees, and it is not from boxing doctors that they will as a rule seek treatment. Therefore I make this suggestion to all those of you who seek the truth. If you want to know the facts about serious damage sustained in the ring, put your questions to neurologists and ophthalmologists rather than to people who can bear to watch the young bashing each other into unconsciousness.

Here is a letter written to me a few years ago by the late Professor

Weve of Utrecht, a world authority on detachment of the retina. He says: "In the matter of boxing I am absolutely at your side. Not so long ago I met with some difficulties because I refused a well-known boxer from South Africa a certificate that he could enter once more in the ring after I had healed him from a traumatic detachment. I have had no less than four world champions with detachment under my care, among them one who had got a detachment in both eyes within a period of three years, both unquestionable traumatic cases. . . . I admire you for attacking the 'most noble art of self defence' that in my eyes is a very brutal show for people with a minimum of brains and heart and a maximum of infantile atavism." Weve's views on boxing were emphatically endorsed by the late Professor Larsson of Stockholm, another foremost authority on retinal detachment.

The chances of a successful result from surgery done to replace a detached retina are reduced in boxers by reason of the other intraocular damage so frequently found in association. Albaugh, who collected twenty-nine boxers' retinal detachments, found that only five appeared suitable for operation, but a successful result was only obtained in one of these five apparently favourable instances.

Although retinal detachment is rightly dreaded as one of the most devastating ocular hazards of the ring, it is only one among a formidable array. Do not seek information about these from the boxing doctors. Look at the relevant ophthalmic literature, in which you will find a fearful catalogue of lacrimal derangement, paralytic diplopia, iritis, cataract, glaucoma, vitreous opacity, choroido-retinal degeneration and optic atrophy. The normal macula, upon which are focused the clear images of objects under direct gaze, is a particularly vulnerable portion of the ocular fundus, and I have examined many boxing victims in whom diminished visual acuity of one or both eyes was amply explained by choroido-retinal pigmentary degeneration, scarring and atrophy in this macular region.

Do not believe the people who pretend that amateurs are exempt from these disasters. Jokl has rightly pointed out that in its reaction to injury living tissue is not influenced by the monetary arrangements between the boxer's managers. No amount of regular medical inspection will alter the fact that the retina is flimsier than a piece of tissue paper.

Eye doctors are, of course, well aware that damage to the eyes themselves is not the only explanation for lowered visual efficiency. The eyes cannot interpret their own images. Interpretation depends upon the intricate ramifications of the visual pathways, and upon the linkage of these pathways with other parts of the brain, that very organ which is the main target for a knockout punch. The infliction of severe, permanent, progressive damage to the brain from boxing has been repeatedly established, and I will not presume to encroach upon ground that neurologists will cover tomorrow, but I have thought it right to stress the close relationship of the eyes with the central nervous system. The proper timing of punches depends upon the state of the central nervous system even more than it does upon a healthy pair of eyes.

Here is a typical boxing word-picture from one of our widely circulating newspapers: "near the end of the sixth round there came a clash of heads and a bad cut opened over Howard's left eye.

"Skilled hands repaired that cut in the interval but it only needed two or three left jabs early in the seventh round to open it again." Here is another: "An injury to McAteer's left eye in the second round caused most of the trouble. It was not possible for me to see definitely whether it was a punch or a butt with the head that led to the wound.

"Humez is a rough customer and he was twice warned in the first two rounds to keep his punches up and for the questionable use of his head in charging in to the attack. . . . A trickle of blood ran down McAteer's cheek from the second round on and the eye became a target for many of Humez's best punches. Before the end it was like a half-opened oyster, and it was plain that he could not focus properly through it." When I hear medically qualified people proclaim that the chances of serious eye injury in boxing are remote, I know only too well that they are not likely to be convinced by argument. They have been given the opportunity to study the anatomy and physiology of our special sense organs, among which the eyes are clearly the most vulnerable; but so blind is their devotion to boxing that they airily dismiss the likelihood of havoc from a volley of punches directed upon the eyes.

We are told that boxing promotes patience and courage, and it is only fair to admit that there is some force in this argument. There are, however, many forms of sport which not only inculcate pluck and endurance, but also allow the participants to triumph without deliberately damaging a fellow mortal.

"Yes," they will say, "but isn't a boxer favourably equipped to deal with thugs and bullies?" Not at all. A thug is not likely to stand in a good light waiting to be hit on the jaw. He is more likely to attack you with a knife from behind. Incidentally, we know that a man skilled in wrestling, judo or ju-jutsu can make short work of a boxer.

Boxing is hailed as an excellent form of physical culture, but there are many athletic pursuits which develop the body in better proportion. Long years in the ring are all too likely to produce a simian, top-heavy appearance, from over-development of the upper half of the body. Another excuse put forward by boxing fans is that they chiefly enjoy the adroit footwork and skilled defence mechanism of an expert boxer. No doubt these discriminatory enthusiasts exist, but Lt.-Col. Farthing, a former sparring partner to Joe Beckett, has stressed the less savoury aspect of those fights. In his view the majority of persons who attend professional boxing matches are not interested in a skilful boxer, who by adroit movements, avoids punishment and wins his fights on points decisions.

"All they clamour for," he says, "is a man with a 'killer punch' and they wait with avid and sadistic anticipation for the moment when it is successfully brought into action and his opponent is battered into submission or sinks unconscious to the floor of the ring."

It may be true, as boxing devotees are fond of proclaiming, that more people have been killed on the football field than in the ring, but surely the total number of football players vastly exceeds that of boxers. Nearly all sports are attended by hazards, and hazards cannot altogether be eliminated, even if we were to wrap people up in cotton wool and put them in a glass case. I wonder what you will think about this specious argument recently put forward by a medical man in the lay press. He said: "Boxing is not the only sport where one opponent deliberately tries to hurt the other." He goes on to speak of ". . . kicking, elbowing, scratching, gouging and even biting that goes on in the rugger scrum, the ankle-tapping and punching at soccer, and the deliberate attempt to injure one's opponent at hockey, polo and lacrosse". Alas, there are foul players in nearly every kind of sport, and in this imperfect world many bad things will escape the notice of a referee. Nevertheless, the man who wrote that letter must know quite well that all the nasty things which he lists are contrary to rules, and will be penalized if they are detected by an honest referee. We should not judge a game by the disreputable tricks of its less scrupulous players. What a howl of indignation he would let forth if boxing were condemned on the score of the deliberate head-butters, kidney-punchers, rabbit-punchers and hitters-below-the-belt. Serious and even fatal injuries will from time to time arise in many different sports, even without intentional foul play, but the deliberate disabling of your opponent is forbidden in ball-games, running contests and most other forms of sport. In boxing the main point is to disable your opponent, and the surest way to do that, if you can catch his chin unguarded, is to concuss him with a blow which may damage him for life or strike him dead.

J. L. Manning has recently pointed out that since 1945 an average of eighteen fighters, professional and amateur, have been punched into their graves every year. "The medical case against boxing," he suggests, "is overwhelming. It remains largely unacceptable in Britain and the United States only because ballyhoo for the next big fights distracts public attention from the sadism of the one before." Manning is a layman to medicine, but we who have been shown the central nervous system and the sense organs in all their beautiful intricacy should be all the more eager to oppose a pastime which wrecks Nature's artistry.

A. RUGG-GUNN, M.B., F.R.C.S.

Consultant Surgeon, Western Ophthalmic Hospital
Consultant Ophthalmic Surgeon, Central Middlesex Hospital

I AM very grateful for the opportunity of discussing in this conference certain aspects of eye injuries said to be due to boxing. I must say, however, that it is rather hard that my matter-of-fact description should follow immediately on Mr. Doggart's graceful and eloquent pleading. The subject is a large one, but I propose to confine myself to what is really a synopsis, firstly on orbital fractures from a purely ophthalmic point of view, so as not to interfere with the material of the Maxillo-facial session; secondly, on the rather obscure relationship of brain trauma to ocular symptoms, which I trust will be rendered less obscure later at the Head Injuries session; and, lastly, some facts concerning retinal detachment.

Owing to their varying density and arrangement in bars and curves the orbital bones are resistant to trauma. I have seen, however, several instances of fracture, caused by accidents apart from boxing, and on two occasions the lower orbital rim was fractured in fights after violent quarrels, and not diagnosed in either case until it was too late to attempt replacement. The result was diplopia, which was easily overcome by prisms, but in one the inferior oblique muscle was affected. Another case had unilateral optic atrophy without any history of fracture, but X-rays revealed distortion of the optic foramen, probably due to fracture of the area between the optic canal and the superior orbital fissure. This patient was a boxer, and on inquiry I was told that, six months before, he had suffered a severe black eye on that side in a boxing bout.

Haemorrhage in the anterior chamber of the eye, often associated with distortion of the pupil, is not uncommon in injuries and usually becomes absorbed. I, myself, have suffered this on two occasions, not boxing. Once I was hit directly in the eye by a rackets ball, and fairly recently by a metal tube, about one inch in diameter and several feet long, blown by a gust of wind. I was wearing spectacles, which apparently prevented serious injury. Dislocation or part dislocation of the crystalline lens is said to occur in boxing, but must be rare. Haemorrhage in the orbit does occur, causing proptosis and sometimes immobilizing the extrinsic muscles. I have been told by colleagues that the clot may become fibrous and continue to restrict movement, and also that some proptosis may remain. Haemorrhage in the optic nerve sheath is more serious. The ophthalmic artery enters the optic nerve sheath in the orbit from below, usually on the nasal side. Once within the sheath it immediately turns at a right angle, or almost a right angle, towards the eyeball, and is prone to rupture by a sudden blow. The result may be strangulation of the fibres of the optic nerve and atrophy. Whether this happens often or at all in boxing I do not know, but it does happen not infrequently in accidents.

Head or brain injuries, either severe and associated with disturbance of consciousness, or relatively mild but frequently repeated, often produce ocular symptoms, especially nystagmus. The neurologist may have little difficulty in localizing the lesion at fault, but the ophthalmologist in examining eyes has been accustomed to rely on the type of nystagmus, when present. Apart from purely ocular defects or lesions, the usual source of nystagmus is the elaborate vestibular apparatus, ranging from the labyrinth to the vesticular nuclei of the 4th ventricle. This relationship suggests a lesion such as a punctate haemorrhage, in proximity to the brain stem, that is, medulla, pons or midbrain, and, as there are several varieties of nystagmoid movements, the different varieties have been accepted by ophthalmologists as a guide to the site of brain injuries. For example, rotatory movements are characteristic of vestibular nystagmus but also occasionally vertical or horizontal ones. Vertical movements on the whole have been considered as pontine lesions, and the coarser type of nystagmus as deriving from the cerebral cortex.

This is not, however, the situation today. Recently, Mawdsley and Ferguson published an excellent study of ten ex-boxers suffering from neurological disease, mostly striate and cerebellar, and eight of these had nystagmus. Exactly twelve months ago Spillane of Cardiff published a most interesting discovery, viz. that four of the five ex-boxers investigated by him, all suffering from organic cerebral disorders, had defects of the septum pellucidum, which were revealed by means of air encephalography. This organ, consisting of two thin membranes, triangular in shape, and separated from each other by a cleft, is situated between the two lateral ventricles, separating them from each other anteriorly. The septum pellucidum can only be seen by the lumbar air encephalogram, which was employed for this purpose first by Spillane and later by Mawdsley and Ferguson of Manchester. The latter investigators found abnormalities of the septum pellucidum in six of their ten patients. It is clear that a new field has now been opened for promising research.

Finally, I would like to add a few remarks on detachment of the retina. Every ophthalmic surgeon has large numbers of cases under his care—in one of the women's wards of the Western Ophthalmic Hospital today five out of fifteen patients have detachments of the retina—and modern methods of operation have become very successful. The occasional examples due to boxing differ from what we may call the ordinary types. The latter usually begin as a tear in the upper periphery of the retina, and gradually the detachments work down to the inferior periphery. In the case of the true boxing type, apparently the result of a series of injuries acquired over a long period of time, ultimately a collection of minute cysts develop in the macular area, and may lead finally to a central detachment. This rare type is less amenable to operative procedures than the ordinary type.

In conclusion, I wish to say that my association with boxing is entirely with amateurs. It happened, however, that when appointed Surgeon to the Western Ophthalmic Hospital, a boxing school for professionals was round the corner, and I saw many cases of injuries to the eyes, including some detachments of the retina. Also, I must make it clear that the great majority of the injuries described in this paper were not due to boxing at all but to accidents. The risk of injury to the eye in boxing certainly seems to be small, but when injury does occur it is often serious.

DISCUSSION

LT. COL. GRAHAM: The first speaker gave rather an emotional account of eye injuries. I know, and many of you here know, that these frightful injuries can occur in boxing. I shall try to show that in actual fact they hardly ever do so. The facts that I am now going to give you are fully documented. Seventeen medical officers of the Board of Control were asked for their experiences in regard to serious eye injuries. They had an average of eighteen years' experience each. Out of 9266 contests which involved 18,532 boxers, there were only seven cases of serious eye injury that were reported by the medical officers who had to deal with them.

The principal medical officer of the French Boxing Federation, Dr. Favory of Paris, a very well-known ophthalmic surgeon, reports that in the French Federation in fifty years they had fifteen. The Italian Boxing Federation, who are provided by a liberal government with money to look after their affairs, have produced an excellent résumé of all boxing injuries over the last ten years, 1952-61. During that time they had an average of 4517 boxers per year registered. During those years they had eight serious eye injuries. These are the findings of our own medical officers, the French Boxing Federation and Italian Boxing Federation. Finally, Liverpool has always been a centre of professional and amateur boxing. I approached a leading ophthalmic surgeon in that area, trained at Moorfields Hospital. I would like to read you his letter:

"I worked at Moorfields Hospital for ten years, three years as R.S.O. Since that time I have been consultant ophthalmic surgeon in the Liverpool area. That part of my experience started in 1941. During the whole of this time since 1930 until the present day I have only seen two bad eye injuries due to boxing. Both of these men had detachment of the retina, both were highly myopic; they should never have been allowed to box. Both these injuries were seen in the early 1930s whilst I was at Moorfields. I have seen three detachments in athletes since I have been in Liverpool. One was in a rugby player, one was in a long-distance runner and one was in a professional wrestler, and these people were also fairly high myopes. I personally have never seen a badly torn lid, neither have I seen an eye so badly hit as to render any permanent injury apart from the two detachments in myopes which I have quoted above."

Ladies and gentlemen, serious eye injuries can occur in boxing. Many of you have seen thousands of contests and know that they are so rare as to be negligible and cannot be regarded as a serious hazard in boxing.

MR. KEITH LYLE: I should like to say how much I have enjoyed listening to the first two speakers and also to the comments of Colonel Graham. I do not wish to be at all emotional about this subject.

As a boy I had to learn to box and I think there is a considerable difference in boxing with schoolboy gloves and the sort of gloves used in professional boxing. As an ophthalmic surgeon it has been my lot to deal with a large number of cases of eye injuries in boxing. Fracture of the orbital margin and orbital haemorrhage are relatively slight and can usually be rectified. Permanent detachment due to damage of one of the retinae may be much more serious.

It was my privilege to have as a patient a world champion boxer. As a matter of fact, following two operations I had cured his double vision. He went back into the ring and not only did he knock out his opponent but he killed him—so there was a fatal accident in the ring.

Detachment of the retina may be a condition which can be successfully remedied by means of operation, but cases due to boxing injury are much more difficult to deal with and results are very rarely so successful as cases of detachment of the retina due to other causes.

The point I would like to make is that repeated trauma to the eye, just as to the brain, gives rise to a form of concussion. This condition sets up fibrosis in the retina, giving rise eventually to gross defects of vision. When I was serving with the R.A.F. in the war, it was my duty to examine a number of professional boxers who wished to be admitted as P.T. instructors. As far as my memory serves me, I think the whole lot had evidence of detachment of the retina. This condition was so severe that it grossly affected a large percentage of these men and their physical ability and most were unfit to be admitted to the service. So many of them were not really aware of their defect; they had come to accept that their sight was not too good and could not be treated by any means at all.

In my experience there are a number of very serious injuries which affect the eye due to boxing and I think we must accept these facts. Some of us are likely to come across more cases than others and there are many ophthalmic surgeons who may not have the experience.

As a surgeon at Moorfields, I would say that we do get a number of serious cases of eye injuries due to boxing.

DR. BLONSTEIN: I am speaking as a senior medical officer of the A.B.A., and the first point I would like to take up is Mr. Doggart's reference to retinal detachment which he said was on the whole remote. As far as amateur boxing goes it is extremely remote. I have been vetting amateur boxers for thirty-four years and during that time we have only had two cases of detached retina. I personally have seen three cases of detached retina in a very short period amongst Scottish rugby players.

As for the other serious injuries he mentioned I say emphatically we do not get these serious eye injuries in amateur boxing. I personally have never seen any. Mr. Doggart talked about football deaths as compared to boxing deaths and he did mention that since 1945 there have been fourteen deaths as a result of boxing in the British Isles. That figure is perfectly correct—nine amateurs and five professionals—but he did not mention the fact that only last year, in 1962, the Registrar-General's official figures gave six boys who were killed playing soccer and eleven young men playing rugger. So, however deplorable these deaths are, the deaths resulting from boxing compare very favourably with such a widely played sport as football, and even cricket. Six boys lost their lives last year. In motor-cycle racing in one week three young men under the age of twenty lost their lives in races this year. Mr. Doggart said the main object of boxing was to knock your opponent unconscious. The object of boxing is to defeat your opponent by out-pointing him, the main object is not to knock your opponent unconscious, although it does occur.

(The Chairman remarked that it was obvious that there was a very considerable difference between the two classes of boxing and perhaps they should be considered under their two headings.)

DR. WILLIAMS: I think we must agree that there are serious eye

injuries which occur in boxing—these are described on the highest
authority, which cannot be disputed. We have also heard figures
suggesting that these are rare. What I should like to ask the experts
is whether there are any statistics which give the rate of risk of these
serious eye injuries in boxing. Recently a paper has been published
on the rate of risk of death in various activities, including amateur
and professional boxing. It was discovered that the rate of risk of
death in amateur boxing would be 450 deaths every 10^9 hours that
amateur boxing went on, the equivalent in professional boxing being
70,000 per 10^9. A death rate of 100 per 10^9 would certainly be acceptable as a risk rate in any activity. An injury or death risk of 50,000 to
100,000 in 10^9 hours would be totally unacceptable. Obviously it is
agreed that there are serious eye injuries in boxing. Is the incidence
of eye injuries in boxing (not the comparative figures with other
sports) high or low? If it is high, can we say that it is acceptable, if
it is low can we say that it is unacceptable?

MR. DOGGART: I do not carry figures easily in my head and I
cannot answer that. It would need complicated statistical research,
it seems to me.

CHAIRMAN: We do not want to spread the field too wide. There is
a measure of calculated risk involved in any activity and if we are
not going to cease to live as human beings we must accept a certain
measure of calculated risk. When one realizes that all these risks
involve a life then I think that point is important and we must try to
give an answer. To live a life without any risks at all would not be
living. If this risk is so small as to be quite negligible as compared
with, say, walking across the road, then I think this puts the thing
in the right perspective.

DR. P. R. SAVILLE: At the outset I would like to say I have every
respect for Mr. Doggart's skill as an ophthalmic surgeon, but I
must say I have never listened to a more unscientific, emotional and
biased talk than his. I was hoping to hear some detached scientific
evidence of the sort given by our second ophthalmic speaker. Whilst
having every respect for Mr. Doggart's opinion on normal ophthalmic matters, I cannot accept what he said. The figures he quoted—
do they come from England? As far as we are concerned, who
control professional boxing in this country, we do not know them
and I am sure they do not come from this country. There are some
countries which have very little control (these countries should have
control) where these things happen; they certainly do not happen

here. To say that the non-boxing doctor or ophthalmologist or neurologist sees all the cases and we do not is, to my mind, a lot of nonsense. It is not just a question of examining a boxer before a fight—these men are followed up and we are in close contact with them. If there are all these cases, surely we must come across them? I note Mr. Doggart made great play on Nelsonism—I would say he is a real case of reversed Nelsonism, if there is such a thing. I would also like to add that in this country each boxer is examined at least once a year apart from the normal pre-fight medical examinations when we look particularly for eye injuries. If there is any lowering of the standard at all the boxer is suspended. We had a case only yesterday where a very well-known boxer whose eyes were lower than our standard (6·9 in one eye and 6·8 in the other) had his licence withdrawn. All boxers' medical sheets are looked at very closely, and over a period of years it is rare that we get any real deterioration in the very short space they continue boxing. In the case of the ten boxers mentioned, if my memory serves me correctly, they were mainly (nine out of ten) boxers of the pre-control period before the Board of Control came into being with its very strict medical regulations. Finally, I would like to say that I originally suggested that we should have one session on the psychopathology of boxers and boxing because I think the most interesting thing would have been on the psychopathology of the opponents of boxing. Today has convinced me more than ever that we cannot find objectivity in certain types of doctor.

MR. C. FRANKS: . . . I came here with an open mind. There are two points which occur immediately after hearing what I have heard. The first makes me suspect the intelligence of the pro-boxing gentlemen who have spoken. I have heard put forward as an argument the fact that six women have suffered from detached retina. That sort of argument is not going to encourage me to favour their side. They have also put forward this other point of injuries in other games. I thought it had been made fairly clear that in other games the injuries are not deliberate but in boxing they presumably are. At present anyway, as one who has come with a perfectly open mind, I am veering against boxing, though I am quite open to be moved the other way if the boxing protagonists can convince me.

MR. MCDOUGALL: I am an ophthalmic surgeon and I look after injuries in soccer and rugby amongst other games, and in the past ten years, amateur boxing. Here I would stress that I am speaking entirely on amateur boxing. We must distinguish between amateur and professional boxing.

In the past ten years I have not seen one boxer with an eye injury that much affected him. Three or four retinal haemorrhages have occurred which resolved completely with adequate treatment.

Mr. Doggart gave a very good outline of all the injuries to which the boxer is susceptible, but not only due to boxing. His remarks were rather emotional and when he states that in other games had the referee seen the breach he would have penalized the man, it is no consolation to the man that had the referee seen the incident his opponent would have been penalized. One feels that the referee must have detached retinae in both eyes to allow the sort of conduct that all of us see in some games.

As a previous amateur boxer myself and as one who takes extreme care and interest in boxing in amateur circles, to my mind the dangers to the eyes have been grossly overstressed as far as amateur boxing is concerned.

Mr. C. Ralph: We have had no schoolboy boxing in Gloucestershire since the war. There are two points on which I should like clarification. It has been said that there is a distinction between amateurs and professionals which has been partly answered by the first speaker. But this is a much more important point—practically every professional boxer was originally an amateur and it is amateur boxing that is providing these bodies for professional boxing. In the same way, amateur boxers come largely from the schools and so it goes on. That is why it is discouraged in my county. The second point is the argument that is always put forward and certain figures have been worked out: that there were six boys killed playing soccer last year. I would suggest that there must have been six million boys playing soccer that year. When anyone draws a comparison, one must take into consideration the number of persons taking part and the length of time they take part. I think this is a very important thing.

Mr. A. J. P. Martin: Mr. Franks has made one remark which I think cannot be accepted by schoolmasters—that boxing is discouraged. We feel that every boy should be given the opportunity to take part in whatever sport he wishes. We are well aware that in schoolboy boxing there must be some control. The schoolboys' A.B.A. is set up not for the purpose of organizing boxing but as a part of physical education, and we do look most carefully into any aspect which can bring hurt or injury to the boy. I am not convinced that eye injury is the result of hitting with the gloves. We have had statistics given to us and I should like to ask how many eye injuries have resulted from the butting of the head rather than from a blow with the gloves. Also from a schoolboy's point of view I cannot see how we aim for this very upper part of the target, the eye. Personally I would rather the target was confined to the part below the head, but apart from that we do encourage boys to use the whole of the target, especially the body. May I repeat, how many eye injuries are the result of a blow with the glove? Or are more a result of butting with the head, which could happen in any other sport.

MR. FRANKS: I would like to make it clear that so far I have personally done nothing to discourage boxing in my county.

LT. COL. GRAHAM: I think I can answer what percentage of the eye injuries are due to the use of the glove or the misuse of the head.

About seven years ago in the Board of Control we had a survey amongst our own boxers and the result was that in the initial stages something like 97 per cent of the cuts around the eye, which are not serious injuries, occurred as a result of the misuse of the head. Subsequently, due to the formation of scar tissue a punch had more effect. Cuts for the second time over the same eye were caused more frequently by the glove than by the head.

Another survey was made by doctors in New York who were provided with means by the New York City authorities over a period of years to photograph at the ringside every contest in slow motion. They produced miles and miles of slow-motion films. I saw some of these films myself and agree that something over 90 per cent of cuts were caused by the head and not by the gloves.

MR. F. J. KEEGAN: As schoolboy boxing has been mentioned, I would like to make one statement in its favour. For many years (I think twelve) we have had with Dublin an inter-cities tournament. We have been to Dublin one year and Dublin has come to London the following year. I asked for the following figures because schoolboy boxing was being attacked in the past year and I wrote to the secretary of the London Schools A.B.A. for these figures. I did this particularly because these contests are amongst the toughest and of the highest standard of any schoolboy boxing. The champions of the London area are up against the champions of the Dublin area and you know what the Irish are like.

There have been 119 contests and in the whole of that time one boy has had to see a doctor, but he was back for a meal with every-body and joined in the celebrations afterwards. As an amateur boxer myself I would like to add point to this business of the causes of eye injuries. If gloves are any good you never get cut with a glove, it is always a head and sometimes an elbow. I have played both rugby and also boxed—I have had two cuts from boxing and two from rugby.

MR. A. V. KNIBBS: I have been mainly interested in schoolboy boxing. I am most interested in Dr. Williams's question on incidence of eye injury. If the incidence is very high (or indeed even if it is low) what can be done about it? Can the medical professions indicate what sort of protection is possible against eye injury, perhaps some sort of protective clothing? Are the administrators of boxing prepared to legislate for protective clothing of the head?

MR. DOGGART: What I would say when replying to most of the people in favour of boxing I have already said in the course of my paper. I do think perhaps Dr. Blonstein is a little confused because he quoted me as mentioning detachment as a remote possibility. I did not suggest that retinal detachment was a remote possibility and I drew attention to it's special dangers in boxing. I have heard Dr. Blonstein's reassuring remarks for many years; he keeps up a stream in support of his pastime. Some of his reassurances have worn a little thin so far as I am concerned. I have often heard them contradicted. I happen to have with me a letter from the *British Medical Journal* written by a doctor in reply to an article in which Dr. Blonstein made the usual reassuring remarks about the rarity or absence of injuries. This was a man who had attended as medical officer over 2000 tournaments, and disagrees with Dr. Blonstein's conclusions.

Dr. Blonstein's reassurances have worn a bit thin as far as I am concerned, but I was not so optimistic as to suppose I could convince him by any arguments of mine.

MR. RUGG-GUNN: As far as cuts of the skin near the eyes are concerned, they are very common indeed. I have known the same men have a cut in exactly the same place half a dozen times in suc-cession, but I can only repeat that I have seen extremely little injury to the eyes themselves as a result of boxing of any sort or kind.

SESSION II

MAXILLO-FACIAL INJURIES

Chairman

D. N. MATTHEWS, O.B.E., M.D., M.Chir., F.R.C.S.

Surgeon, University College Hospital
Plastic Surgeon, Hospital for Sick Children
Pastic Surgeon, Royal Masonic Hospital
Civilian Consultant in Plastic Surgery to Royal Navy

3

MAXWELL ELLIS, M.D., M.S., F.R.C.S.

Surgeon, Royal National Throat, Nose and Ear Hospital
Surgeon-in-charge, E.N.T. Department, Central Middlesex Hospital

THE somewhat romantic accounts of prize fights of long ago make interesting reading, but the stories of these bouts lasting up to 100 rounds, fought with bare fists and including a certain amount of all-in wrestling, leave something to the medical imagination. For my own clinical interest I would have welcomed a description of the injuries received, especially those sustained by the nose. The knuckles must have become terribly battered hitting against hard skulls, but this might only have hardened them for the lesser encounter against the nasal bones. However, while the pugilist could breathe through his mouth (what happened when the jaw was broken?) and had sufficient remaining functioning ribs to move his thoracic cage, one presumes that the mere flattening of a nose was scarcely worth recording.

In the modern professional prize ring one sometimes reads sickening accounts of ploys designed to win contests. Apparently the clashing of skull against eyebrow in a deliberate attempt to split it is part and parcel of the game. Amateur boxing as conducted in this country under the control and by the rules of the Amateur Boxing Association is a very different matter and the safeguards on which they insist keep boxing within safe limits which are acceptable in other sports. Among the most sensible provisions are the limitation in the number and length of the rounds, and the weighting and padding of the gloves. Both operate to prevent serious injuries. It would take an extremely strong person to inflict serious bone damage with these gloves, and the shortness of the round is an additional safeguard, as any injury comes quickly under medical inspection and the medical officer has the unquestioned power to stop the bout. It is true that the sole motive of a boxing bout is the infliction of injury, but this is often also the underlying motive in modern football and cricket, especially as played at international level, where it is rarely checked either by authority or public opinion. The punch-drunk boxer has received a great deal of sympathetic attention from the Royal College of Physicians, but I have yet to meet one, and he scarcely exists among amateur boxers. However, I have sometimes met his equivalent in ex-rugby football players, sometimes in circles which have astonished me by their loftiness and importance.

I have very little to say about the emergency treatment of the nasal injuries for I do not believe that ringside measures are often successful. Lacerations of the nares or free epistaxis are reasons for stopping the bout. Cold compresses to the nose may deal with epistaxes, but pinching hard between the fingers as much of the nose as can be seized and maintaining the pressure for several minutes is often a more successful first-aid measure. An adrenaline spray can be effective, as can a pack of ribbon gauze or wool soaked in adrenaline. Lacerations are best cleaned and covered with a sterile dressing and the boxer sent where the wound can be accurately sutured. A timely manual manipulation may occasionally reduce a fracture immediately after it has been caused, and is perhaps worth trying in what appear to be suitable cases. The bout should always be stopped and cold compresses applied and the boxer advised to continue them frequently. He should be referred for further treatment as soon as possible, which will probably be the next day, as most boxing contests occur in the evening. Reduction should be performed as soon as possible after the infliction of the injury, although it is fairly readily possible up to fourteen days. After this, disimpaction of the fragments may demand a vigorous and even a hazardous degree of violence. The presence of swelling is not relevant to the ease or otherwise of reduction, but, as the swelling subsides, the retaining splint will become loose and must be replaced by another after three or four days.

What major injury can the average amateur boxer's gloved fist inflict upon his adversary's nose? I see a number of cases where damage has occurred, as a good many are referred to me at the Royal National Throat, Nose and Ear Hospital. The nasal bones are occasionally fractured, but much more often the septum has borne the brunt. Depending upon their normal relative variations in size, the inferior half or three-fifths of the septum is unprotected by the nasal bones and is vulnerable to direct trauma. The punch can be squarely on the target or alight on it from one or other side. The extent of the injury is thus governed by the degree and the direction of violence and also the amount of unprotected septum.

Laterally applied force may dislocate the septum from its seat on the maxilla, pushing it to one side. Sometimes the cartilage also cracks along the line of curvature into which it is bent by the blow. Occasionally the ethmoidal plate also snaps across vertically. In the late teens or early twenties the bone is usually relatively elastic and may bend momentarily and then recover its shape rather than break, but the degree of violence clearly plays a determining part. If the ethmoidal plate does break, the anterior portion of the septum then swings across like a door.

More direct frontal violence may produce a number of different deformities all based on the production of crumbling injuries. The bony portion of the septum, chiefly the ethmoid and vomer, snaps across in varying places depending on the direction and force of the blow, whilst the cartilage may buckle or break if its elasticity is exceeded. The fragments take up positions dictated by the causative trauma. Sometimes these fragments slide alongside one another, producing a thickened septum, whilst at other times they become angulated.

When the blow has been sufficiently strong to break the nasal bones, the septum is invariably fractured at the same time and the fragments are dragged into positions governed by the final position of the nasal bones.

The net result of these various injuries ranges from virtually nothing on the one hand to severe cosmetic deformity on the other. Sometimes, however, when neither the appearance nor the function are affected, epistaxis may later occur with the slightest trauma. This is a particularly annoying symptom as a cause is rarely found. I believe it might be due to stretching of the mucosa over a minute break in the septum or nasal bones, one too insignificant to attract attention clinically or radiographically. The least trauma might cause sufficient movement to break the mucosa and start bleeding. This condition is particularly annoying if the origin is not discovered, as an otherwise fit and good boxer may have to discontinue the sport for a relatively trivial reason.

In the usual way the treatment of nasal injuries varies with the degree of deformity or displacement. Quite often, a nasal bone fracture can be seen in an X-ray with the fragments in good alignment and with no external deformity or internal obstruction. No active treatment is necessary. If the nasal bone fragments are angulated, reduction is necessary and the sooner after the injury this is

3

performed the better. The usual principles in reducing fractures are observed, and the instrument commonly used is Walsham's forceps. The final position may be relatively stable and require no fixation. Usually, an external plaster of Paris splint is necessary, sometimes combined with intranasal packing. Half-inch selvedge edge ribbon gauze impregnated with bismuth cream or bismuth iodoform paraffin paste (BIPP) is a convenient packing material and can safely be left in place for several days. If there has been much comminution, the reduction may be unstable. A steel wire mattress suture is inserted in a horizontal plane through the nasal bones, passing in close to the maxilla and out near the bridge line, or in a vertical plane, transfixing a small lead plate placed over each nasal bone, passing in close to the maxilla and out near the bridge line, or in a vertical plane, transfixing a small lead plate placed over each nasal bone. When this suture is twisted to the right degree of tension, the comminuted fragments are held in position. The suture should be left for a fortnight.

Severe injuries producing a dish-face deformity are scarcely ever encountered in amateur boxing. The difficulty in treatment is to keep the reduced fragments in position. It is often necessary to wire the nose as described previously, and maintain elastic traction in a forward direction from a forehead harness mounted on a plaster of Paris head-band.

Fractures of the septum alone are treated along the same lines. No treatment may be necessary, but when the cartilage has been cracked it is often difficult to manipulate it back into position and even more difficult to retain it there. Packing in each nasal cavity, using half-inch ribbon gauze impregnated with BIPP or bismuth cream, may suffice, or through-and-through sutures may be needed. Fragmented cartilage unites by fibrous tissue and has an unpleasant tendency to slip back out of alignment, but bone throws out callus which helps in fixation. Where severe cartilaginous fragmentation or bending has occurred, fixation by through-and-through suturing maintained for many weeks may be the only way of obtaining a good result.

All nasal fractures, like fractures elsewhere, should be corrected as soon as possible after they have occurred. If this early opportunity has been lost, it may not be feasible to manipulate the fragments back into alignment, and if several months or years have elapsed, surgical rhinoplasty will be necessary if there is much cosmetic deformity. If, however, nasal obstruction is the residual disability, where the septum has borne the brunt of the violence, operation on the septum alone may be sufficient. Often a combined procedure is necessary, and this is best performed at one and the same operation.

Restoring an airway obstructed by a septal deformity is one of the oldest rhinological operations, and techniques have progressively improved. In submucous resection the mucosa is separated from one side of the septum and the obstructing cartilage and bone dissected away from the mucosa on the other side and removed. The two mucosal surfaces then come together more or less in the mid-line. The resection of bone and cartilage weakens the septum and thus the nasal bridge, and once performed increases the difficulty of a subsequent rhinoplasty if this should become necessary. In fact a bone or cartilage graft or a plastic prosthesis may be required to straighten or hold the bridge line. The modern reposition operation is more logical although often more difficult to perform. The bent septum should be straightened by reversing the original violence. Very bent and twisted portions are removed. The septum is then manipulated back into position. With experience and a little ingenuity, and sometimes force, a satisfactory realignment is always possible. The position must then be maintained until the fragments are solidly united. This type of operation does not impair the strength of the septum and can be combined with a rhinoplasty.

I have not mentioned or described compound fractures, as these are rarely encountered in boxing. However, they can occur when the nose strikes against the rope-supporting poles or the floor of the ring, or sometimes against the opponent's head. The various positions of the fractured bone and cartilage are then complicated by skin wounds. I have found it convenient to clean the wounds first of all, then perform the reduction of the fractures, finally suturing the wounds and applying the requisite type of fixation.

These methods of treatment are the routine ones which would be used for injuries occurring in ordinary life. When occurring in a young boxer, the ideal treatment must often be modified by other considerations. If impairment of the cosmetic appearance and function are minimal, there is a case for no treatment at all, especially if the boxer is at the beginning of his boxing career, and even more if he shows promise and is likely to do well competitively. It is more than possible that a further nasal injury will occur which might even restore the original condition. If, however, a first or second injury causes a disability which would ordinarily need active treatment, there are still, in a boxer, some practical points to consider. Can he go on boxing satisfactorily without treatment? If this is at all possible, it is desirable, because of the risk of subsequent injury rendering nugatory the effects of treatment at this stage. However, whether or not treatment should be withheld must remain a matter of judgement, and perhaps even of opinion. Advice can never be dogmatic and must be based, as before, on a number of non-surgical considerations.

If reduction is considered necessary, boxing should be forbidden for two months to allow of proper consolidation before risking further injury. Using the methods briefly outlined earlier the structure of the nose should not be weakened.

When treatment has not been advised, and in case minor traumata worsen the position, the boxer must be examined every few months for reassessment, until his boxing career is over. The appropriate surgical treatment to remedy the deformity and functional disability should then be given, or at any rate strongly advised.

4

B. N. Bailey, M.B., F.R.C.S.

Surgeon, Plastic Surgery, Jaw Injuries and Burns Unit, Stoke Mandeville
Hospital

Facial injuries occur frequently in amateur and professional boxing because the face is interposed between the gloved fist and the brain, which is one of the chief targets. Facial injury is unlikely to prove fatal, and with the exception of severe eye and nose injuries does not cause loss of function in the amateur. The professional is differently placed in that repeated facial injury may result in long periods when he is unable to box, and to the premature termination of bouts.

Prevention of boxing injuries is desirable so long as the purpose of the sport is not lost. However much devotees decry the necessity for knockdowns and knockouts in boxing, violent physical contact— its avoidance where possible and its endurance where necessary— are the heart and soul of boxing. This, of itself, rules out the use of complete protection as used by American footballers. Protection of some tissues is accepted, and gum-shields and protective boxes should be worn.

Boxing gloves that present a supple unbroken surface reduce the risk of facial abrasions and lacerations. The practice of kneading the padding away from the knuckles of the glove should be stopped. Careful cleaning of gloves after a boxer has been down should replace the perfunctory wipe on resiny trunks.

Contrary to the belief of some trainers, there is no way to toughen facial skin. Sun lamps, brine baths and tea compresses may promote a feeling of security but have no effect on the durability of the skin.

High standards of refereeing to prevent the deliberate use of the head in professional boxing, and ignorant butting in amateur boxing, will reduce the incidence of cut brows. The referee who stops a bout the moment one of the contenders becomes incapable of defending himself incurs the displeasure of the crowd, but may well save a fractured jaw or head injury in the final knockout.

Amateur treatment by corner men should be discouraged. In the early rounds of a professional bout a cut over the eye or a severe bruise round the eye will be played upon by the opponent until such time as the eye is closed or covered with a sheet of blood. By the time the referee stops the fight—with or without reference to a doctor—a skin-deep laceration which could, with proper treatment, heal with a minimum of scarring becomes a contused, deep, infected gash plastered with quack remedies by the "cut-man". This may be a source of recurrent trouble for the rest of the boxer's career.

Failing prevention, early expert treatment immediately after infliction of an injury is the likeliest way to prevent recurrence.

The common facial injuries in boxing are: (a) cauliflower ears; (b) general facial bruises, abrasions and cuts; (c) bruises round the eye; (d) lacerations of the eyebrow and eyelid; (e) cuts of the lips; (f) fractures of the mandible and teeth.

(a) *Cauliflower ears*. A blow which traps the external ear against the unyielding temporal bone may tear a blood-vessel which allows a pool of blood to strip the perichondrium and skin off the cartilage. Deprived of its blood supply the cartilage necroses, and it is distortion of the cartilaginous skeleton plus the thick subcutaneous plaque of organized haematoma which gives the boxer, wrestler or rugby forward his tin ear. The only adequate treatment is early evacuation of the blood by a small incision through the posterior skin under local anaesthetic. When the haematoma has been expressed, its recurrence is prevented by packing the ear with cotton wool soaked in liquid paraffin. The object is to apply a soft mould to all the concavities of the ear, and then apply a firm *crêpe* bandage over the top of this. The paraffin wool hardens and maintains the shape of the ear, and by its pressure prevents the reaccumulation of blood or serum and holds the skin against the cartilage so that it can revascularize. The dressing should be worn for ten days, and boxing can be resumed after two months.

Later on, cauliflower ears can only be treated by a tedious and not very successful operation under general anaesthetic where an attempt is made to shell out the thickening.

(b) *Bruises and abrasions*. These are the price a boxer has to pay for being struck in the face. A dab of any mild antiseptic fluid followed by exposure of abrasions is all the treatment required. Bruises cannot be prevented, and it is doubtful if there is any effective cure.

(c) *Bruises round the eye.* The skin of the eyelids is soft and redundant. The subcutaneous tissues are tenuous and the blood-supply copious. The outcome of these factors is periorbital haematoma to the pathologist—a black eye to the boxer. It is not possible to influence the amount of swelling, which depends on the laxity of the skin and the size of vessel damaged. There is no external application —raw steak, ice bag or astringent lotion—which influences the swelling in the slightest degree. This is painfully apparent in plastic surgery where we are unable to prevent bilateral black eyes after operations on the nasal bridge. It is equally frustrating in an eyelid operation to place one of the last stitches through a subcutaneous blood-vessel and produce a black eye. You may be assured that if there were any method to prevent black eyes—we would adopt it.

Various substances have been used to prevent and treat haematoma and oedema. Blonstein used prophylachtic streptokinase and streptodornase in one set, and dummy tablets in another set of boxers and compared the results. He formed the impression that there were less haematoma and contusions in the treated series than in the control group. Streptokinase is reputed to act by hastening the removal of the fibrin barrier which forms round any tissue damage. Whether or not it does this, it is impossible that it should prevent the formation of a haematoma or contusion as these are purely dependent on the mechanical tearing of a blood-vessel. It may hasten the resolution of a haematoma, although objective proof of this is very hard to obtain.

Chymotrypsin (a proteolytic enzyme) has been enthusiastically advocated by Moore who claims more rapid dispersal of haematoma and oedema—though their initial formation is unaltered. Gall and Talbot found no reduction in post-operative bruising or oedema, and Calman and Barr also report negative results after carefully controlled trials in a wide variety of facial operations.

(d) *Cuts round the eye.* Cuts below the eye are relatively unimportant, and a boxer may be allowed to carry on the bout with a laceration of the cheek. Cuts over the eye are in a different category because the supero-lateral orbital margin is sharp, and cuts in this region tend to be deep and gaping and because gravity causes blood to trickle over the eye and impair vision.

Many eye cuts are caused by the clash of heads and could be avoided by stringent refereeing. Others are due to the bony configuration round the eyes, and in this respect certain boxers are unfortunate in having sharper ridges than others. A perfectly fair punch with the knuckle of the glove will compress the skin against the sharp orbital margin and cut through it. This happens even more readily when there is already scar tissue in the region from previous cuts.

Once an eye is cut the fight must be stopped. There is no treatment the corner can apply which effectively stops the bleeding. Local adrenaline constricts small blood-vessels for a time and allows easier clotting of blood. Styptics of various sorts are used—but judging from the frequency with which patients with bleeding tooth-sockets continue to knock on the door of casualty departments, they are ineffective. How much more is this the case when the damaged part, having had a minute's rest, is subjected to a barrage of blows aimed at provoking swelling and stimulating haemorrhage.

The cut eye must be treated with care from the start as this is the only chance to get first intention healing which is necessary if recurrence is to be prevented. In a hospital under good lighting, with aseptic conditions an expert should repair the cut. If the amateur boxer is not prepared to wait for proper treatment he may accept a few quick stitches—and the possibility of recurrence. The professional boxer would be most unwise to compromise. He must receive the highest standard of surgical care for the cut eye, which, more than any other facial injury recurs throughout his career if inadequately treated. The amateur boxer—who has in any case only to survive three 2- or 3-minute rounds, can afford a long lay off, give up boxing completely, or take the risk of recurrence while his professional counterpart cannot afford this luxury.

The method advocated by the British Boxing Board of Control —using a hypodermic needle—is useless for anything other than a skin-deep split, and the possibility of using elastoplast dumb-bell sutures round the eyebrow and eyelid is remote.

Any wound requires (a) haemostasis, (b) toilet and (c) closure in depth, to avoid dead space in which a haematoma will form and to minimize the gap which will be bridged by weak fibrous tissue. Haemostasis can only be achieved under hospital conditions and must be complete. After it has been achieved the wound should be irrigated with hydrogen peroxide to clear residual clots out of the depths, and if there is no recurrence of bleeding the wound should be closed in layers. Use non-chromic 5-0 catgut to unite the deep layers, and insert the stitches upside down so that the knots are buried. If these stitches are properly inserted there will be no cavity left beneath the skin, and the skin edges will be lying almost together. The skin should be united with 6-0 monofilament nylon threaded on atraumatic needles. The stitches should go vertically through the skin, less than a millimetre from the edge, and should be 1–2 mm apart. Antitetanus serum or toxoid may be administered according to one's convictions or current fashion. Skin stitches should be removed after forty-eight hours and if it is possible a strip of ribbon gauze soaked in collodion placed along the freshly healed cut to splint the edges till healing is secure. Boxing is banned for three months.

The boxer who has had inadequate early treatment or is cursed with extra sharp orbital margins or super-ciliary ridges may have a mass of scar tissue and paper thin skin, which splits with the first blow. This condition may be remedied by removal of the entire scar, smoothing off the bony prominences and providing a pad of dermis to add resilience to local tissues.

(e) *Cuts of the lips.* These should not occur often if properly fitted gum-shields are worn, but from time to time the mucous membrane of the lip may be split by a direct crushing between glove and teeth or gum-shield. A split of quarter of an inch or less will heal rapidly without stitching, but over this size a few fine catgut stitches under local anaesthetic will give better apposition and quicker healing.

(f) *Fractures of the facial bones* (with the exception of the nose). These are most uncommon in boxing. McCown quotes the injury rate for a seven-year period of 11,173 boxers in New York State. There were 1010 facial lacerations and contusions and four jaw fractures in this series. Five hundred and seventy-five bouts had to be stopped due to soft-tissue injury, and many of these were recurrences. The relative importance of fractures and lacerations is shown by these figures. Rowe and Killey quote 500 peace-time fractures of the facial bones treated at Rooksdown House, and find that only two were due to boxing.

Fracture of the mandible is a rare occurrence only likely to occur in the late stages of a hard-punching professional bout—the more so where one of the contenders is on his last legs with open mouth and slack jaw. Under these circumstances a powerful hook may fracture the condyle neck on the side opposite the blow. A direct blow to the point of the chin is transmitted along the mandible to the tempero-mandibular joint, but in the young adult with normal dentition and occlusion most of the force is expended in the molar region where it is transmitted to the maxilla.

The unilateral condylar fracture is apparent by pain and tenderness over the tempero-mandibular joint, a feeling of incorrect dental occlusion and trismus. No first-aid treatment is required, and after X-ray confirmation of the diagnosis, the teeth are wired together for a month. Boxing may be resumed in three months.

Less commonly, fractures will occur at the angle of the mandible and in the canine region. These are self-evident with severe pain, dental malocclusion and trismus, and are again usually treated with interdental wiring. If support for the jaw is required, a single turn of 3-inch elastoplast under the jaw and over the top of the head is superior to the barrel bandage. A tooth is occasionally loosened, and if its pulp is undamaged it may be wired to adjacent teeth until it becomes firm again. Major dislocations are nearly always accompanied by torn apical vessels, and to avoid infection and staining of the tooth a pulpectomy and root-filling should be performed. A tooth completely dislocated may occasionally be replaced after root-filling, though it will not always take, and in any case will only last for a few years. Fractured teeth are always painful, and when broken at the crown may be temporarily filled and later depulped and root-filled. Teeth fractured across the roots need X-rays for diagnosis and are likely to be lost.

The condyle head is the chief centre of manibular growth, but even the rare, high intracapsular fracture which occasionally separates the epiphysis completely from the rest of the bone does not usually give rise to disturbances in growth. Fractures at the condyle neck which do occur in boxing do not give rise to disturbance of mandibular growth because of the excellent blood-supply to the head of the bone. There is no evidence to suggest that the repeated trauma of boxing will affect mandibular growth.

Sport injuries in general deserve expert attention—not the grubby ministrations of untrained self-styled physiotherapists, masseurs and manipulative specialists. In boxing, we would see a reduction in the incidence and recurrence rate of facial injuries by using only the best equipment, by strict refereeing, and by ready access to expert medical treatment.

DISCUSSION

MR. D. B. BILLIMORE: Is the injury sustained by a boy or a young person likely to be more serious to him than to someone of greater maturity? Is the rate of recovery slower or quicker in boys or young people?

DR. WILLIAMS: Granted perhaps that plastic surgeons have a vested interest in the proper management of facial injuries in boxers, I would like to ask a question of both speakers, bearing in mind the criticism Mr. Bailey has made of the method of suturing a cut eye advocated by the Medical Sub-committee of the British Boxing Board of Control. What would you like to see (a) set out in legislation, and (b) set out in recommendations by the boxing authorities regarding the proper management of a cut eye?

DR. BLONSTEIN: I would like to point out to Mr. Maxwell Ellis who talked about bouts lasting 130 or 140 rounds, that in those days a round ended whenever the boxer went down. Very often the round might only last a few seconds. I was interested in the remarks on fractured noses and fractured jaws: in the A.B.A. we keep statistics of these injuries. In a series of 6000 senior contests held in the season 1962–3 we had only three fractured noses. I would like to ask Mr. Maxwell Ellis if he can give us an idea of the percentage in other sports and in civilian life.

I would like to ask Mr. Bailey about broken jaws. As far as the A.B.A. is concerned, in the 6000 contests we only had two fractured jaws during the 1962–3 season. Mr. Bailey made reference to the administration of tablets such as Varidase, as prophylactics and for treatment of bruises and haemorrhages, etc. I introduced this particular product for use in the United Kingdom and we in the A.B.A. have had excellent results with these preparations. We have reduced the amount of bruising by 15 per cent and haematoma by some 50 per cent. If boxers take this preparation for three or four days after receiving a bruise or a haematoma, these clear up very much more rapidly. This has been our general experience and most amateur boxers under the auspices of the A.B.A. now ask for this preparation, particularly if they receive a haematoma.

CHAIRMAN: First, we should consider the very important question of the influence of age on injury and the influence of age on the speed of recovery from injury and the extent of recovery. It is a very important aspect with facial injuries when boxing itself is a sport which is begun very early in childhood and must, therefore, be of extreme importance to all those responsible for social clubs, boys' clubs and so on.

We have been questioned about legislation and recommendations regarding cut eyes and the percentage of injuries of the nose and other soft tissues for other sports and civilian life. This is pretty difficult to answer. Mr. Maxwell Ellis said, I think, that if a boxer sustained an injury (he quoted displaced fractured septum) this should be repaired forthwith by a surgeon with special skill in this kind of work. How soon does he think it would be safe for the boxer to start boxing again and on what criteria would he judge? Mr. Bailey said that a cut over the eye necessitated a boxer taking three months away from boxing before he started again. What advice would he give to a boxer after suturing a recurrent cut over the eye? Is a recurrent cut to the eye sufficient justification for advising a boxer against continuing or should he have a longer spell off boxing before he resumes?

MR. MAXWELL ELLIS: There is no doubt that in young people all the tissues are more elastic and more resilient. To this extent they are much more likely to bend than to break with the same degree of violence. If an older person and a young person sustain the similar degree of violence to the same area, then in a younger person the nasal bone or gristly septum will certainly tend to bend rather than break, whereas in a person much older it would bend up to a point and then crack across. The bony points of the nose will be much more likely to bend than break in younger people. This is purely relative and if the violence becomes more severe, then in either a young or an old person the break will occur when the limit of bend is over. If under a blow the septum begins to bend in this way, at what point would this cease to bend? This will depend on its elasticity and up to a point is a direct reflection of age, being more elastic in younger and less elastic in older people. The repetitive bruises in younger people are more variable than in older people. In the age group with which we are concerned, people about fourteen to twenty-eight-thirty, the relative nature of this becomes a little theoretical. In all these people the reparative processes are more active. This raises points. For many years it has been said that if a child (a little boy of six, seven or eight) falls over and bashes his nose he may sustain a nasal fracture which is not discovered although a few months later it is quite clear that he has a nasal deformity. It has been said that it is better to wait until this child has ceased growing and then by some plastic surgical procedure make this ugly nose better. The theory is that if one interferes with the bone structure, one would interfere with the proper growth of the nose. For the past ten years there has been a school of thought, of which I am one, that it is wrong to delay and that this deformed nose should be straightened as soon as possible and these bones put back in their proper position.

Let us introduce the general proposition of a fractured arm or leg or any other bone. Nobody says you must not set these fractures until the child ceases to grow. The centres are probably well away from the fracture and if we put these bones back in the right position, the growth will be rather better. I hold that in the same way with the nasal fracture, the sooner the nasal fractures are repaired, the better, and the nose will grow to its proper size ultimately. Taking this point therefore to its logical conclusion, I would say that in young people the reparative process should be certainly more vigorous and you would expect a very rapid degree of healing and growth, and, therefore, a more rapid degree of deformity if the deformity is not reduced at an early stage. In the process of growth, if the columella of the nose is in the wrong shape or position as the boy grows, so his nose will grow progressively more ugly and deformed and more inefficient. I therefore do agree that although the likelihood of damage is perhaps less in a youngster and that his reparative processes are much quicker, when damage does occur it is even more important that it should be put right at an early stage.

Dr. Blonstein raised the question concerning the length of the round, pointing out that the round ended with a knockdown, but nevertheless these bouts did go on for hours—the whole morning or afternoon might be spent—and when you consider how rapid our modern bouts are when heavyweight boxers get knocked out in 2 minutes, one wonders what this is all in aid of! Is this commerce or an expert technique which did not exist in the days of old? The important point was that the longer a bout lasted, the more likelihood of damage there was.

With reference to the broken nose and cut eye, if damage occurred during the bout then that injury was likely to be made worse because of the length of time it was being battered. This is, I am sure, something to do with the stability of repaired cut eyes; we shall hear more about that later. My own feeling is that the bout should be stopped immediately once the eye is cut and the cut should not be "doctored" by the seconds. The bout should not be allowed to carry on until it is clear that the person with the cut eye cannot continue. The more bruising of the area, the thicker the scar tissue. In the 6000 contests in which three broken noses occurred, if you examined these figures carefully this is 0·05 per cent. Although I have no figures, I said that broken noses in amateur boxing were rather rare, and this is confirmed if a boxer only manages to cause such fractures three times in 6000 bouts lasting an average of two to three rounds. How very safe these heavy gloves must be compared with the physical efforts of the people wielding them. Take rugby football; there is not a season in which a boy does not get a nasal injury or fracture of some kind or another, probably undiscovered. One realizes the number of injuries of this kind that must have been sustained in this particular game. When you think that here are 6000 bouts, the nose must be deliberately hit quite a number of times. Think of the number of times in civilian life in which you meet broken noses (it is quite considerable, apart from the large number which never come up for treatment and are only noticed in passing). It must be considered that this is quite astounding when the hazards of falling over a mat and bashing one's nose are almost greater than fighting in a boxing ring against someone who is determined to hit your nose. Three only in 6000 bouts and I would have said that it was a great deal higher in rugby and in other sports like riding, etc.

The length of time after the repair of a nasal injury is a little bit of a guess. One knows that in about a fortnight a nasal fracture has become so tightly stuck together that attempts to reduce are often unsuccessful. In a fortnight after reducing a nasal fracture, nature has got going on her side of the repair. One would say that in a fortnight the bones are reasonably well knit together. Give it another fortnight and bones must be practically back to square one from the point of view of stability. How will it stand up to a punch? I generally say you can go back in a month or six weeks, playing for safety, as it were, but I have no real knowledge about this. A month is probably on the short side, six weeks should be ample for the nose to be able to stand up to the sort of violence to which it is subjected in the ring.

The cartilage, however, does not heal at all well—a great deal less well than bone does. The septum cartilage is the part that stands up least well and heals with more difficulty and probably takes a longer time over it. Damage to a nasal cartilage is not in itself necessarily a reason for stopping somebody boxing if he is good at it. If the nasal cartilage were the only point at issue the boxer could be allowed to box on and have it mended when he has finished his career. In amateur boxing you are only boxing for fun and you can be redirected to other sports. There is not the commercial problem there. There is no reason to subject anybody to unnecessary risks.

MR. BAILEY: As far as any small child or younger person is concerned I should have thought the inflicting force is correspondingly weaker. In the case of small boys boxing or fighting one must realize that the chance of damage is very small up to the age of about ten or twelve. During the adolescent period there is slightly more liability to have well-developed boys causing some sort of injury when delivering accurate blows. The nasal framework is more resilient and the ability to promote cuts is not so well developed in the adolescent as in the mature man. The only possible site where injury might be more severe would be at the neck of the mandible which does not fuse until the eighteenth or twentieth year. The condyle could be so disrupted that the mandible would fail to grow on that side.

As far as healing is concerned, I do not think that within the large group we are considering there is very much evidence that it is better than at any other time of human life. Although apparently less effective as one gets older, repair is a matter of the activity of individual cells and these do not themselves get any older. To say that tissues respond less well at a later age is not strictly true. As far as bony growth is concerned, since it is more actively growing in the young, healing may be better than at a later period. There is no increase in the healing power in soft tissues in the younger patient as opposed to the older patient.

With regard to cuts there is no question that you have to adopt elaborate measures. You have simply got to say that without exception a fight will be stopped when a cut appears over the eye. Otherwise this reduces it to a matter of human judgement and puts pressure on the person who is to make the decision. If the eye is cut, it will be made worse by the opponent; you must say categorically that a cut eye should stop the fight. There is no moral stigma attached to the referee or boxer. The fight having been stopped, the patient should then be sent to the casualty department of the nearest hospital where the cut should be properly stitched by someone who is capable of doing it. This is not necessarily a plastic surgeon—anyone with adequate skill or adequate instructions is capable of doing it.

Dr. Blonstein referred to the question concerning two fractured jaws in 6000 contests. I have got no figures to answer this with and I agree this is a very good record. My own impression is that, in the course of the year, I deal with far more jaw fractures in football and rugby players and water-polo players than in boxers.

With regard to Dr. Blonstein's comments on the use of Varidase, there is no method of stopping the bruise from developing unless there is some already present deficiency in the blood-clotting system of the body and you cannot clot broken blood-vessels. You cannot make it disappear sooner until the tissue is healed. As far as causing the resolution of haematomas are concerned, there is really nothing that is effective.

MR. MATTHEWS: In the case of the recurring "cut eye" injury it would be ideal if the patient came along seeking definitive plastic surgery. You would completely cut out the scar tissue and try to give him a fresh fine scar. Although one might say six months instead of three months for subsequent convalescence, there would be no real reason for prolonging it. If somebody came along with a recurrent injury which is liable to have to stand up to a prolonged strain in that region, you might be more cagey about sending him back more quickly, but since you would be reducing the amount of scarring I do not think that, unless you are doing anything more complicated (such as trimming the supra-orbital ridge), you should give him more than three months off boxing. For the simple repair, three months should be sufficient.

SESSION III

HAND INJURIES

Chairman

BRIGADIER H. L. GLYN HUGHES, C.B.E., D.S.O., M.C., M.R.C.S., L.R.C.P.

Director, South-east London G.P. Centre
Medical Officer, British Red Cross Society

5

RAYMOND FARROW, B.M., B.Ch., F.R.C.S.

Consultant Orthopaedic Surgeon, North Middlesex Hospital
Surgical Tutor, St. Bartholomew's Hospital

INJURIES to the hand and wrist resulting from boxing are not common, but when they do occur they are exceedingly important in this respect, that pain, swelling and deformity are not outstanding features and, therefore, these injuries are very likely to pass recognition.

They fall, as I see it, into two main groups. First, those that result in a faultily delivered blow (or a faulty block to a blow) and second, those that result from a trip and a fall, where a boxer falls on an outstretched hand, injuring the wrist rather than the hand.

Now the hand in boxing in a glove bears no resemblance whatsoever to the clenched fist of open fighting. I have X-rayed some willing boxers in their gloves with fist clenched as tight as it could be, and the metacarpo-phalangeal joints are only flexed to about 50–60°, with the fingers slightly open, and the thumb almost straight and abducted from the side. This is due largely to the fact that the hand has to grip the palm of the glove, and therefore is more open. Due to the splinting effect of the thumb encasement, and the fact that the padding on the side causes the thumb to be a little on one side, the thumb, if it is not held close into the side of the glove, is placed in a position of maximum vulnerability, and therefore it is most liable to injury. For, as it is abducted from the side, and as it is more or less straight, it is liable, if caught on the end to have the force of the blow transmitted as a piston straight the way down. As you probably know, the base of the metacarpal of the thumb sits on the trapezium just like a man astride a horse, with a leg on either side. If the force coming down on to the saddle is sufficiently great then one of the legs is broken off, and the whole of the thumb can then shift downwards, as it were, on the sides of the horse. As it is an injury which is not particularly painful, and there is very little swelling to reveal

43

its presence, it is most likely to be missed on examination of the hand. The most dramatic feature of it is this, that as the whole thumb has been shunted downwards by the force of the injury, so it can easily be pulled back without a great deal of pain, and as soon as it is released it will of course shift back again.

If the thumb is allowed to remain in the wrong position, then of course the function of the carpo-metacarpal joint will be impaired for life, and within the course of a very short period of time a gradual but steady loss in the range of movement—together with an early arthritis of the area and considerable pain—will occur, requiring, almost invariably, eventual arthrodesis of that joint, fixing the thumb, which should be the most mobile digit on the hand. The other fingers then have to take on some form of gripping movement towards the thumb, which is a grossly inadequate form of function. Therefore, in order to bring the rider back into the saddle and to fit the leg that he left behind accurately into place, it is absolutely essential, in a joint of this nature, for accurate anatomical reduction. In the ordinary course of events, this is not too difficult because all you have got to do is to pull it back and into place, but that pull must be maintained, otherwise, if it slips at all, mal-union will occur. There will be a step in the articular surface, and as a result of that the articular surface of the trapezium will be worn away very rapidly, with all the complications that I have already mentioned. The easiest possible way of doing this is, as you see in the course of examination, to pull on the thumb. You then have to maintain that pull. The easiest way is to enclose the arm in plaster and then fit in that plaster a metal bar, coming out to provide something against which the pull can be made. When that is all in place and properly moulded, then a very short general anaesthetic of gas and oxygen is all that is required in order to drive through a small pin or stitch through the pulp of the thumb and then with a piece of string connect it up to the bar which is incorporated in the plaster. It is the easiest possible thing to do and one of the most successful forms of treatment, and it is always the treatment of choice.

Now there are a lot of people who, rather than take the easy straightforward method, would try and invent a clever method— and there is a clever method going round, and its results are almost universally bad. So a word of warning against it is necessary, and that is this. Once the thumb has been pulled upward and manipulated into position, then it will lock into that position. While it does that in the majority of cases, the accuracy of reduction is never as good as by linear traction. This method has the added disadvantage that, unless it is done by an expert who has got the feel of these things and knows just how hard he can press and how hard he cannot press, then when the plaster comes off after three weeks, there is going to be a point of pressure here and a ragged dirty plaster sore with the radial artery lying at the bottom of it. Also, the function of the thumb, due to the fact that the tendons have been burdened and have become adherent, is permanently impaired. This is a dangerous method of treatment and one never to be recommended, except perhaps for those peculiarly skilled in its use.

Now in a small proportion of Bennett's fracture dislocations one may be satisfied with the fact that one has overcome the displacement, yet the leg is not fitted back completely on the rider, and this is invariably due to the fact that there is some soft part intruding, or a small fragment of bone that is keeping it apart, and unless that is treated by open reduction then the results will be just as bad as if the thing was not reduced in the first place. The method of open reduction, which was devised by some Danish surgeons is now beginning to be used in this country.

Bennett's fracture dislocation, as it is rightly called, can be treated up to some weeks after injury. Therefore unlike some of the others, immediate and expert treatment is not always an essential. The raw end of the bone is, of course, in contact with articular cartilage, and therefore no attempt at union occurs, and the thing remains as mobile as it would do on the first day of fracture. The results do not differ at all in the first three weeks, but, providing accurate reduction is obtained and maintained for about three weeks until the union has occurred, the results are excellent in every case, and late osteo-arthritic changes do not occur when the complete congruity of the joint has been restored. Untreated or badly treated (either with failure to overcome the shortening, or failure to fit the fragment back in place) these fractures universally end with exceedingly bad function and very great pain in later years, and considering that young men who do this are going to require that thumb, not only to achieve their prowess as a boxer, but also to earn their living for another forty years, it is essential that the accurate anatomical reduction should be obtained and no inferior results be accepted.

The next injury to the thumb, and the only other common one that occurs in boxing, is an angulation injury again, which may result from blocking the blow or sometimes a fall in which the metacarpo-phalangeal joint is angulated. Due to one or other the (usually) medial collateral ligament is ruptured. That may be visible on an X-ray in view of the fact that it is pulled off with its insertion into the base of the metacarpal. Too often this is just called a chipped fracture. It is not a fracture in the true sense of the word at all, it is a complete avulsion of the collateral ligament, and must be properly treated if complete instability of the joint is to be avoided. More often than not, however, there is no avulsion and the ligament is snapped in the middle, in other words through soft tissue, and nothing is visible on X-ray. It is always accompanied by true dislocation with immediate self-reduction, or spontaneous reduction, and like all true dislocations it must be treated as one, not merely as an incidental chipped fracture or something of that kind. The whole of the capsule of that side must be allowed to unite together again and to heal properly before use is allowed. On examination you will find, although sometimes difficult to elicit to start with, that the thumb will, on passive movement, come right out sideways without the slightest difficulty, and as in all true dislocations, it is not particularly painful when one does that. Incomplete dislocations and sub-luxations with intact capsule are of course always exceedingly painful immediately afterwards, but these injuries are not, because everything is torn and therefore there is nothing much to cause pain when the deformity is reproduced by passive movement. This injury must be allowed to heal otherwise in all the complex movements of the thumb used under power, the articular surfaces of the metacarpo-phalangeal joint will become incongruous and, therefore, wear will occur. There are quite a large number of people in whom I have had to arthrodese this joint because twenty years later they have had extreme pain and stiffness of the joint, interfering with the earning of their living and interfering with their night's sleep, all resulting from this type of injury.

When it comes to the rest of the hand, there are only two other injuries that occur at all commonly in boxers. Surprisingly enough one would not think the mallet finger would ever occur in a boxer, and yet it is one of the commoner injuries the mechanism of which I am quite at a loss to explain. I always thought it would be due to a training accident, with a person punching against a bag and mistiming his punch and still having an open hand, but in all the ones I have seen it has always been sustained during the course of a competition or contest. You all know what it is—the extensor expansion on the distal phalanx is ripped from its insertion and if untreated can become very painful for a long period of time. One must remember its anatomy to a certain extent, in that it is not just an extensor slip going to the base of the terminal phalanx, but constitutes the whole of the dorsal capsule of the joint, and therefore the joint itself is laid open on the dorsal surface and pain and swelling are correspondingly increased. There are two main types, one in which rather like the collateral ligament of the thumb, the expansion has snapped in its soft part, and one where the insertion has been ripped off. The joint is merely hyper-extended in order to allow union to occur, usually over a month or six weeks, and held in a hyper-extension splint of some sort or another—there are hundreds described (everyone describes his own). The results in those are pretty good, usually about 80 per cent full function, because bony union takes place. But in the mallet finger in which the expansion is torn across and no bone is injured at all, the result is universally poor and certainly under 50 per cent union, with the result that when the splint is taken off in about a month or six weeks you find that once the stiffness is overcome either the expansion has not healed, or it has become stretched and some permanent deformity results. If, after about four to six months that deformity is no longer a painful or a tender deformity it requires no further treatment for, except in expert violinists (and guitarists now, I suppose) the injury confers no disability on the hand because the position of full extension of the finger, although elegant, is seldom used in the working of the hand, and flexion deformity does not interfere with it. Very occasionally people either continue to have a lot of pain or they maintain they have a disability, and then only should operative reduction be undertaken. It is an exceedingly difficult thing to do from the technical point of view, because the bone at the base of the proximal phalanx is very friable and it is liable to break very easily when one is dealing with it. It is exceedingly difficult to stitch a bit of shortened extensor expansion back on to a bone which will splinter very easily as soon as any attempt is made to pass a needle through it in order to hold the suture.

So much for the mallet finger. The fourth boxer's injury of the hand is, of course, what is sometimes called by boxers the "stove-in knuckle" or angulated fracture of the neck of the metacarpal. Following angulation the head of the bone begins to point downwards. This is an exceedingly important injury to treat properly, because the disability conferred upon the function of the hand if it is not treated properly is very great. By fracturing the neck and tilting it down, the whole joint is tilted down as well as the fractured fragment, and therefore even though the patient does achieve full extension in his metacarpo-phalangeal joint after union, full extension will still only bring about 30 degrees up to the normal extent, and that is an exceedingly annoying deformity to have. The finger continually gets in the way when one is merely putting one's hand in the pocket for loose change or a handkerchief, let alone trying to earn one's living, and it is therefore essential that this angulation is corrected into the normal anatomical position. The method is perfectly simple and perfectly safe, and yet it is so seldom undertaken. The collateral ligaments of the metacarpal-phalangeal joint, as you know, are arranged in such a way that when the fingers are extended they are perfectly lax (if they were not you would be able to open out your fingers) but when the metacarpo-phalangeal joint is flexed to 90 degrees they become taut as evidenced by the fact that if you put your hand in that position you cannot open the fingers as you can open them when the fingers are extended. As these ligaments become taut in flexion then once the finger is flexed one has, through the finger, complete control over the fractured fragment of the neck of the metacarpal, and therefore the treatment is perfectly simple. The finger is flexed, then pressure is applied to the proximal phalanx, and because the head of the bone is held perfectly by these taut ligaments on either side, it can be shoved back into position and held there very easily just by the forearm plaster worn until union has occurred. After that there is no long-term disability in that finger. Even if it is only a few degrees it is still a nuisance, because always that person is trying to get it straight, and will therefore put undue tension on the anterior capsule and cause himself pain by stretching the capsule.

There are only two other injuries that I want to mention. They occur in the wrist, and they result usually from a fall or a boxer being hit savagely on the forepart of the wrist when he is off guard completely.

The first is displacement of the lower radial epiphysis, and I stress this one because it is one of the injuries that may so easily pass recognition. Boys up to about sixteen years of age suffer the injury (seldom later than that because the epiphysis is usually beginning to fuse by then). The boy suffers the injury and it is immediately painful, but within a minute or so the pain has largely disappeared, and there is just a little tenderness in that area and no more. Because the epiphysis shifted up to about a third to a half of its depth in the dorsal direction there is always a little swelling associated with it, and therefore, the step that is made and so easily visible on an X-ray is not easily visible to the naked eye, nor is it easily palpable, and for this reason it frequently passes recognition, sometimes for quite a considerable time. If it is to be treated it has got to be treated within the first day or so, otherwise it is impossible to reduce. Therefore, it is of the greatest importance that boys who suffer such an injury should have an X-ray in order to exclude the dorsal displacement of the lower radial epiphysis. If it is untreated and allowed to remain so then without any shadow of a doubt premature fusion of that epiphysis will occur. It does not matter a tremendous amount in a boy of sixteen years of age, but in younger boys, who are beginning to take up boxing (twelve–fourteen years of age) if premature fusion should occur, that arm has still got two-thirds of an inch to grow, and no growth will take place at the lower radial epiphysis, but growth will take place at the lower ulnar epiphysis and the hand will be forced over in a radial direction, requiring at a later date excision of the lower end of the ulna with all the attendant complications that follow it. Therefore I must stress again the importance of X-raying the wrist to exclude this. Reduction is simple and safe. All you do is to put your thumb on it and push it back, and it stays back and it does not re-displace, needing only a plaster splint to relieve pain.

The other not commonly recognized wrist injury of boys and young men is the fracture of the scaphoid. Indeed, there are a good many textbooks in which it is said that fracture of the scaphoid does not occur before adult life. Nothing could be further from the truth. It does occur and it is not an uncommon injury, and therefore there is no such thing as a "sprained wrist" until such time as X-ray and sometimes repeated X-ray has proved that there is no bone injury. The scaphoid may be fractured across the waist, and in about one-quarter of all cases avascular necrosis occurs with failure of union of the bone, so therefore it has to be treated with considerable respect. It is quite frequent for the bone to be broken across its waist without there being X-ray signs of fracture (the fracture line being so fine that it cannot be seen) even using four projections. It therefore becomes of the greatest importance that should a boy or young man have suffered an injury which has caused him pain in the area of his scaphoid (it is never nearly as well localized as the books suggest that it is and there is not much limitation of movement) and in which an X-ray reveals no fracture still continue to complain of pain for a week or so, then that wrist must be X-rayed again. With the passage of time (a week or two) the fracture itself will become slowly decalcified as a result of the traumatic inflammatory reaction which accompanies every fracture, and therefore will become visible on an X-ray film. So let me stress once more that these injuries are not characterized by what one would popularly regard to be the signs of severe fracture, yet the majority of them are severe injuries. Let me also stress that there is no such thing as a sprained wrist until repeated X-rays have been taken to exclude the dorsal displacement of the radial epiphysis and the fracture of the scaphoid.

In conclusion let me finally stress that although these hand injuries are not common in boxing they are very important and demand the utmost care in their management if subsequent disability is to be avoided.

6

WING CDR. C. B. WYNN PARRY, M.B.E., D.M., M.R.C.P.,
D.Phys.Med., Royal Air Force

R.A.F. Principal Specialist in Physical Medicine

WHEN I was asked to contribute to this conference and read a paper, I analysed all the cases of hand injuries due to sport that I have treated during the past fifteen years and found that few of them have come my way from boxing. I do not, therefore, feel that I am competent to give an authoritative paper on the management of hand injuries due to boxing. However, in those hand injuries that do occur, the principles of management are the same as the principles that obtain in the management of any injuries to the hand, through whatever cause.

I would just like to make a few points which we found to be of importance if good function is going to be obtained. First of all, although the injuries are not common, they are very important because a hand is a most important part of the body. Too often in the past (and still in many places today), because the hand is small and because the X-ray of a fracture of the hand looks rather small and trivial, the management of such a condition is left to the most junior staff of the hospital. It is, in fact, much more important to get the most senior and most experienced man to look after a hand injury.

The injured hand, unless it is treated very delicately and very carefully, with very specialized attention, does badly. But, provided it is correctly managed in the early stages with fractures properly reduced and immobilized, and given adequate and skilled rehabilitation afterwards, the result should be extremely good. It is very important, as Mr. Farrow has explained, to obtain accurate reduction, careful immobilization and correct position after any fractures. It is equally important that the patient should have the benefit of adequate rehabilitation afterwards. Now the majority of simple fractures do not require much rehabilitation other than simple exercises under skilled supervision for a reasonable time. The more complicated ones, particularly the thumb fractures, do require more specialized treatment and the importance of the rehabilitation is that the patient should not be allowed to go back to boxing too soon.

There are three major points in the prevention of disability after hand injuries that I would particularly like to stress. First of all, the longer you immobilize a joint in the hand the more likely it is to be stiff permanently. Secondly, bad positioning in plaster can be devastating and, in fact, we regard it as criminal. The one thing you must never do, except in very exceptional circumstances, is to immobilize the hand in a straight position. If you immobilize the hand with the metacarpo-phalangeal joints straight for any length of time you will end up with a frozen hand and extremely poor, if any, function at all. The third thing is, as I have stressed, too early return to the activity—in this context, boxing. It is terribly important that the soft tissues should be allowed to heal, that the joints should regain a full range of movement and that the muscles should become really strong and the patient should have confidence in his hand before he goes back to boxing. This will mean adequate assessment, careful observation by the rehabilitation team and adequate training before being allowed back to competitive sport. I think this is extremely important and often neglected.

From the point of view of the after-treatment I do think that all sportsmen do deserve the best skilled treatment that there is available because their function is going to be that much more demanding than the average person.

There are a few points I would like to make about the management of some of the conditions: first of all, one of the most damaging things after injuries to the hand is the soft tissue swelling. This can so easily, if not managed properly, lead to fibrosis, permanent stiffness and the condition of the frozen hand. It is most important to spot swelling in the early stages in rehabilitation and to prevent it by elevating the hand at night, and making the patient go round in a sling with his hand in elevation, because the slightest bit of oedema, if allowed to persist, may organize and this produces devastating results. In this context we find that the application of ice-packs is extremely helpful in the reduction of swelling and more efficient than heat.

Finally, if one is so unfortunate as to have to deal with somebody who has a stiff hand after either bad immobilization in a bad position, or too-long immobilization, or severe injury resulting in great stiffness, then it is most important that such a patient should be given the opportunity of having full-time, skilled, intensive treatment to get the joint stiffness away, and this will involve serial plaster stretches or a massage—the full gamut of skilled rehabilitation to get these joints back to full function.

I would just like to sum up what I have said by pleading for (1) regarding the hand as extremely important and taking it very seriously, (2) getting the most skilled treatment, both surgical and postoperative, and (3) realizing that the function of the hand in this sort of sport is going to demand so much that it does require the most specialized and greatest care in management.

DISCUSSION

LT. COL. J. W. GRAHAM: As you know, boxers are allowed a certain amount of tape and bandages with which to protect their hands. Recently, in the British Board of Control we have reduced the amount of tape and the amount of bandage—we now allow 3 feet of 1-inch wide zinc oxide and 9 feet of soft open-wove bandage. We are always up against lay trainers in the Board of Control just as the Amateur Boxing medical men are. Lay trainers very often will ignore for as long as they possibly can skilled medical advice. Since bandages and tapes were allowed we thought we ought to advise managers on the best way of applying bandages and tapes because in many cases (and particularly in smaller promotions up and down the country) bandages and tapes which were primarily intended to protect the hand, were used as weapons for offence inside the broken glove. For those of you who do not know, a broken glove has the padding pushed away over the knuckle part of the hand. We found that some managers were building up the amount of tape allowed over the knuckles and with the amount that was going round the wrists and the squashing away of the padding over the knuckle part of the glove they were getting what is pretty well a knuckleduster instead of a glove. We intend, of course, to stop this. I shall be talking tomorrow about that. The application of what is allowed has been quite a matter of dispute even among the medical men attached to the Board. I myself have asked the opinion of a number of orthopaedic surgeons and I have come to the conclusion that we would be very much better without any tape at all. I am not an orthopaedic surgeon and I would like to ask our speakers this afternoon if in their opinion bandaging does protect and if it does, can they say what is the best way of applying it and for what reason? If it is to be applied, in my opinion it should only be applied round the wrist. I have seen many hands that have been damaged by the mal-application of tape bandages. I know of one or two stables where there have been whole crops of injured hands. When I have examined the method of applying tapes and bandages, I have found they have been put between the knuckles, then spread over the top and elsewhere, so that if the hand hits the jaw or the top of the head with any force it is bound to suffer. I personally should be quite happy to see the abolition of tape altogether. Whether that is the view of our speakers I do not know. This, however, is what happens in professional boxing—9 feet of soft bandage and 3 feet of zinc tape. Inspectors of the Board inspect all the bandages, and any tape put over the knuckles must be removed.

MR. W. FLETCHER: From the point of view of amateur boxing, as a layman I quite agree with Colonel Graham that the application of the tape which the professional boxers use causes more injuries to the hand than anything regarding an incorrect blow. Broken gloves are definitely not allowed in amateur boxing. We also have a bandage inspector who sees that the boys' or men's hands are correctly bandaged with the soft surgical or *crêpe* bandages. There is another point—I do quite a lot of university boxing and there we advocate no bandages at all, the padding on the glove is adequate and they are people who have got very soft hands. The amateur boxer has an 8 oz glove against a 6 oz professional.

MR. F. J. KEEGAN: I have always been interested in this question of hand injuries because in the days of long ago when I was an amateur boxer we were not allowed to wear bandages. Then later, soft bandages were allowed. I am personally convinced that bandages will prevent many injuries of the hand from which boxers suffer. I stand to be corrected over this, but I think that in hitting many people hurt their hands because they hit with the outer part of the hand rather than with the middle three knuckles. They have not been taught to avoid hitting with the thumb or outer knuckle not in line with the axis of the arm, and therefore are liable to injury. If you have no bandages on your hands and you have to punch off the other man hard, then, however skilful you may be, you cannot help at some time catching the bone of his forearm or his elbow or his head, and I do not think there can be sufficient protection unless you are allowed to have bandages. But I think soft bandages, properly applied (the boxer always applies them himself), would prevent a great number of injuries.

DR. BLONSTEIN: It is rather interesting that Mr. Farrow should talk at length about Bennett's fracture—most textbooks and orthopaedic surgeons will tell you that it is known as the boxer's fracture. In the A.B.A. that is not our experience. We find that we have more fractures on the second metacarpal than the thumb. I have given you various statistics today, but here are some more. The London A.B.A. figures for the last three years show that in 4350 contests there were three fractured metacarpals; I would like to ask Mr. Farrow how this compares with other sports and civilian life. As far as bandages are concerned, we used to forbid the use of bandages in amateur boxing but since we have introduced the *crêpe* type of bandage there is no doubt that the number of hand injuries has been reduced. We had quite a number of sprained joints without an actual fracture—these were quite common. Since we introduced this type of bandage (no tape) we certainly have reduced the number of sprains. Incidentally, on one occasion we found on inspecting a boy's hand (which rather shows the mentality of some of the boxers themselves) that he had put a visco-paste bandage on his hand which had set quite hard and was just like a fist covered in plaster of Paris!

MR. COWAN: I was extremely interested in Mr. Farrow's description of hand injuries and particularly of ulnar collateral ligament injuries in thumbs. I see quite a number of these and those that have been treated in plaster I find are still frequently unstable when they come out. I have operated on a number as acute injuries and after the skin is incised synovial fluid comes out and there is a complete capsular tear as well. It seems the logical thing just to go in and repair it. Incidentally, I think a similar thing applies to ankle injuries as well. As a result of repairing these, a very simple operation to the injury has proved extremely satisfactory.

WING COMMANDER T. N. N. BRENNAN: To extend Dr. Wynn Parry's comments on the actual incidence of injuries to the hand in the R.A.F. I cannot give you anything on the hand alone but we have got figures for the upper arms and shoulders for 1961–2. Accidents to the upper arm were 1·3 per 1000 and the average stay in hospital or sick quarters under treatment before return to duty was twelve days.

SURGEON COMMANDER J. WATT, R.N.: Our figures are different. During the three years from April 1959 to April 1962 we had a total of forty-two cases of injury to the hand as a result of fighting. Sixteen were due to organized boxing and twenty-six to fights ashore. Again, we found this so-called Bennett's fracture a rather unusual injury, and out of the organized boxing groups we had five with Bennett's fracture and the others were fractures of the metacarpal, usually the neck of the fifth. So far as fights ashore are concerned we had only two Bennett's fractures and the rest fractures of the metacarpals—of the 4th and 5th and also the 2nd and 3rd which we did not see in boxers. They had an average of twenty-one—twenty-eight days outpatient treatment except for those involved in fights ashore which were a little higher. The only cases which went over four weeks were those with fractures of the scaphoid or gross soft tissue injury. I would support Wing Commander Wynn Parry about the importance of starting treatment before gross oedema has occurred as we found that these cases were longer off work when that was allowed to take place.

MR. R. FARROW: Taking the matters in reverse order, the figures from the Royal Navy, as one expects, are higher in hand injuries than any other Service, possibly because they hit harder in the Navy. That the incidence of Bennett's being very much less in the fights ashore bears out what we were saying. You are fighting with a bare fist which is properly clenched. This cannot be done in a glove. With regard to the repair of the ulnar ligament of the thumb, as a primary procedure it should be immobilized in plaster and carefully examined after three weeks when the plaster is removed, and then repaired, if there is any instability present, which there often is. If instability can be demonstrated at the time, then the logical thing, provided you have the facilities, is to go ahead with the repair as a primary measure.

For every fractured metacarpal one sees in domestic practice, other than sporting practice, one cannot estimate the many thousands of people who had had the same injury but have not come up for treatment. Fractures of the metacarpals other than in boxing are exceedingly common fractures as they are exceedingly uncommon in boxing, so one must leave it at that. When it comes to bandage and tape, I do not think I am going to be an awful lot of use to you. I cannot see how they can protect if soft bandage and tape are used as a buffer or alleged support (and a support it can never be, for no *crêpe* bandages can support the force behind a well-delivered punch). One has first a glove and some skin and tissues all of which are movable. One has then added bandaging which is also movable and a tape which I should have thought increased the mobility of that new layer as a whole. The skin is elastic and if shifted returns to its place. Bandage is not elastic and it can easily get out of place and stay out of place to cause knuckle pressure on the fist as the blow is delivered.

5

I must stress my interest is rather more in the treatment of the injuries once they occur and not so much in the way in which they do occur. I have not had a very great part to play in that, but it has always struck me that bandaging is something that the boxer likes to have done to his hands before he puts them into his gloves. Whether it is because he really feels it gives him support and lessens the blow and reduces the likelihood of damage to his hands or whether it gives him that extra fillip that he needs before a bout, I do not know. I have always been suspicious that bandage is of no great value and is a possible danger. Its value is that the boxer can look at it and this is not terribly helpful!

WING COMMANDER WYNN PARRY: I agree with Farrow about bandaging and taping. I think they are of as much value as an elastic stocking round a knee or an iodine locket.

SESSION IV

HEAD INJURIES

Chairman

Dr. Michael Ashby, M.A., B.M., B.Ch., M.R.C.P.

Physician, Whittington Hospital
Neurologist, New End Hospital and Archway Hospital Group

8

(Summary)

A. Dickson Wright, M.S., F.R.C.S., D.T.M. & H. .

Surgeon, St. Mary's Hospital and Prince of Wales Hospital

THE brain is a very wonderful organ, and it has an equally marvellous system for its protection against injury. First of all, it lies within a hard casing—the skull—which protects its delicate substance from all but the hardest knocks. Within the skull, between it and the brain itself, are the three membranes or meninges, between which are two cushions of fluid—the cerebro-spinal fluids. The brain floats in these fluids like a sponge in a bath, and the fluid is constantly renewed and flows from one part to another through small openings resembling thus the shock absorbers of a car. In addition, between the lining of the skull and the surface of the brain run delicate filaments which lightly tether the brain in place and prevent it from swirling about too much when the skull is struck with a blow. The brain itself is thus buffered in the bath of fluid in which it lies, and although it may move a little under the shock of impact it is really very well protected. Injury to the brain itself is thus not very likely under the force of a boxer's blow, even though the blow tends to rotate the skull as well as displace it off centre. What does happen sometimes is that some of the delicate little filaments may be stretched and torn, and as they often have blood-vessels running near them this may lead to bleeding. This bleeding can be a very serious matter, but this is not an injury to the brain itself. In these cases the blood may leak out into the cerebro-spinal fluid and mix freely with it, but if in greater quantity, will not do so and a clot forms. As a result, increased pressure inside the skull does harm by displacing the brain inside the skull.

Another form of intra-cranial haemorrhage which may follow injury, usually a more severe injury such as that due to striking the head on unprotected corner stanchions or the floor of an unpadded ring, is one where the blood leaks out between the skull itself and the membranes. This type of haemorrhage is caused by damage to one of the blood-vessels on the inside of the skull and is well localized, and if dealt with quickly is easily remedied.

These injuries are rare in boxing but they are very important. If they are properly treated they can be dealt with satisfactorily. The reason why some people may die from such injuries is because they may not have been treated properly. I well remember a case of a boxer who sustained one of these injuries—an intra-cranial haemorrhage. He was treated by a young doctor of limited experience who operated on him but could find no bleeding. After the operation the patient got worse and I was called to see him. It was too late, and the patient died. He had got some bleeding but the doctor was not experienced enough to find it. The reason why these injuries are often lethal is because the best individual care is not always available. These patients should only be treated by people of great experience.

One of the objections to boxing raised by many people is that it leads to "punch-drunkenness". We will be hearing a lot about this. The great difficulty about the punch-drunk syndrome is that it comes on late in life, after the boxer's active career is over, and it might not be due to the boxing itself but to the other risks in the boxer's life. Punch-drunkenness used to be fairly common in the old professional boxers and everybody said it was due to the boxing, but you must remember that many of the boxers in those days came from conditions of poverty—they had to fight in order to make a living, and there were, and I should think still are, many temptations for the boxer, particularly the successful ones. These temptations include wine and women. I remember attending to a very well-known boxer once who had neuro-syphilis, which can produce a clinical picture very like the punch-drunk syndrome. You all know that many boxers when they retire become publicans, and certainly many in the old days at least, drank to excess and became chronic alcoholics. The chronic alcoholic may become a person very like the punch-drunk person, and very often it is difficult to say which is which. There are also many harmless things which people do which cause brain damage. The heavy smoker with chronic bronchitis who wakes the whole house with his coughing every morning may be causing little tiny brain haemorrhages of the kind said to occur in the punch-drunk, every time he coughs. There are many other ways in which the pressure in the blood-vessels of the brain may be raised causing then little haemorrhages. In these days, when there are fewer professional fights, punch-drunkenness is almost unknown. Even in cases which do occur it is difficult to be sure that they are due to boxing and not to some other aspect of the boxer's life.

Of course there is some danger in boxing, but then there is danger in every worthwhile sport. You cannot go through life without an element of risk of some sort. The element of risk in boxing is not sufficiently great to justify doing away with the sport. Every sport could be eliminated on this basis. I have even known a player die from injuries received at billiards!

9

(Summary)

Dr. Macdonald Critchley, C.B.E., M.D., F.R.C.P.

Neurologist, King's College Hospital
Physician, National Hospital for Nervous Diseases
Neurological Physician, Royal Masonic Hospital
Consultant Neurologist to Royal Navy

Despite assurances to the contrary, there is little doubt that many boxers enter the ring with the intention of securing an unequivocal verdict by rendering the opponent unconscious, usually by a blow to the head. Inevitably, therefore, boxers are liable to suffer neurological damage which may at times be severe, although it must be admitted it is usually apparently slight and transient. However, it does appear that there is a cumulative effect of multiple neurological disturbances received in the boxing ring leading either, from a short-term point of view, to the "groggy state" or, from a long-term point of view, to the punch-drunk syndrome.

It must be said that the mechanism of the cerebral knockout remains unclear. Sometimes loss of consciousness is acute following a single heavy punch to the head or the concussion of the head on the floor matting, ring stanchion or some hard part of the opponent's body. In the case of the acute loss of consciousness it is possible that damage to the neural tissue itself is slight, although exceptionally it may be severe. A blow of the severity necessary to cause instantaneous loss of consciousness may be sufficient to damage other intra-cranial structures with more or less disastrous consequences. The cumulative effects of blows not in themselves sufficiently powerful to render the patient immediately unconscious may lead to the so-called "groggy state". In this condition the patient, although remaining on his feet, is disorientated, hypotonic and helpless, becoming little more than a passive target for his opponent. It seems likely that if the bout is allowed to continue when one of the boxers is suffering from the "groggy state", severe damage will follow. It is, therefore, necessary for the referee to be constantly on the watch for the first signs of this condition, stopping the fight immediately they appear.

Probably the most important neurological consequence of boxing, however, is the so-called punch-drunk syndrome or dementia pugilistica. I prefer to call this the chronic progressive traumatic encephalopathy of boxing; a somewhat lengthy term that is both descriptive and explicit. This condition tends to be a late sequel to boxing and its manifestations may not show themselves until after the boxer's career is concluded. Once it appears it is slowly but steadily progressive. The presenting features are diverse, often making for some difficulty in diagnosis although it is, of course, to be suspected when the stigmata of the ring (cauliflower ear, thickened supra-orbital margins) are visible. Differential diagnosis is between Parkinson's disease, General Paralysis of the Insane, and frontal tumour. The patient usually complains of headache, dizziness and disturbances of vision. Intellectual impairment is seldom obvious to the patient, although relatives will notice changes in personality with euphoria, fatuousness and defective emotional control. There is frequently a correlation between the degree to which the stigmata are manifest and the severity of the dementia. On clinical examination the usual findings are extra-pyramidal signs.

This condition is much more common in professionals than in amateurs (though it has been described in amateur boxers) and is more common in Whites than Negroes. The class of the boxer will frequently determine his liability to this condition since it is much more commonly seen in second-raters who make up for lack of skill by aggressiveness and a tendency to "slog it out".

The great problem of this condition is that it is extremely difficult to diagnose in the early stages; the commonest early signs include failure to win bouts which the boxer would normally be expected to win and an inordinate recovery period required after the fight. The ability of the "punch-drunk boxer" to absorb further punishment in the ring is disputed; some seem to have a raised threshold, being able to take progressively more and more punishment before going down, while in others the opposite occurs. These latter are sometimes said to be "glassy jawed".

The morbid anatomy of the punch-drunk syndrome is uncertain. The changes described include progressive cortical atrophy, internal hydrocephalus and gliosis. In some cases rupture of the septum pellucidum has been described. These changes are, of course, similar to those in extreme senility. It appears that the progress of the disease is relentless. It is not yet certain whether it can be arrested if boxing is discontinued at the appearance of the first signs. Certainly we must regard this condition, albeit becoming less common, as extremely serious and a very heavy price to pay for a career in the ring.

Boxing is not without danger, least of all danger to the brain. Fatalities are regularly recorded, the causes of death being remarkably varied. It is not so long since three fatalities were recorded in teen-age boys. In some of these cases the cause has been intra-cranial haemorrhage and it is sometimes discovered that the skulls of these boxers are abnormally thin. So serious is the risk of injury, and so peculiar is boxing (in that it is the only sport in which competitors deliberately set out to inflict injury upon their opponents) that there is ample justification on medical grounds for its discontinuation.

10

(Summary)

E. J. Radley Smith, M.S., F.R.C.S.

Surgeon, Royal Free Hospital
Neurosurgeon, Royal National Throat, Nose and Ear Hospital

As a neurosurgeon I inevitably see many cases of head injury, but it is very seldom indeed that I see one due to boxing. While preparing this paper I analysed cases of head injury admitted to hospitals with which I am connected, and the results shown over a period of years are, in other contexts at any rate, certainly revealing. It seems clear that as far as we are concerned very few cases of head injury in boxers are admitted to hospital. This means, of course, that the relative size of the problem is not great, or so it would appear. I must admit, however, that the figures shown are by no means conclusive.

In the first place it may be that there are not many halls or other places where boxing is practised in the catchment areas of the hospitals concerned. If this was so it is not surprising that not many boxers were admitted.

I am quite sure that a second factor is that the way in which head injuries in boxers are treated leaves much to be desired, although boxing is not the only sport to blame in this respect. Players are concussed in rugby and association football and many other games and sports, and too many who sustain relatively minor head injuries from which they apparently quickly recover are allowed to continue with the games. There is much to be said for introducing the count of ten on to the football field and sending off for the remainder of the game any player who is knocked out for 10 seconds or longer.

When a boxer, or indeed any games player, is knocked out he should be removed to hospital on a stretcher for proper observation for at least 24 hours. I know that the majority of boxers who have been knocked out are allowed to go home almost immediately after-

wards, and few I am sure have any subsequent follow up—at least in
the early stages. They do, of course, in most cases have to be checked
over at some later date before they can box again. I do not suggest
that in practice this leads to a great deal of harm being done because
obviously much more would be heard about it if that were the case.
Nevertheless, such concussed patients should ideally be admitted, and
if they were we should see the incidence rate of such injuries more
accurately reflected in the hospital in-patient statistics.

HEAD INJURIES AT THE ROYAL FREE HOSPITAL

Year	Traffic accidents	Drunkenness	Assaults	Falls	School playgrounds	Sport	Cerebro vascular accidents and fainting	Boxing	Building	Other causes	Total
1958 ..	39	7	18	23	2	5	1	0	5	4	104
1959 ..	46	7	17	40	8	5	1	0	6	2	132
1960 ..	30	8	23	28	7	6	1	0	4	7	114
1961 ..	33	7	21	45	3	9	1	0	3	8	130
1962 ..	53	12	29	47	3	17	1	1	3	9	175
1963* ..	20	2	10	24	2	2	0	0	4	8	72
Totals ..	221	43	118	207	25	44	5	1	25	38	727

* January to September.

The figure (44) in column seven, is composed of: basketball 1, rugby 2, football
10, swimming 2, skating 1, riding 3, cricket 4, hockey 1, judo 1, slides 3, swings 16.

It certainly seems that the vast majority of boxers (and patients
generally) who have been knocked out appear to recover completely
and to be left with no bad after-effects—the incidence of complications both immediate and remote does seem to be very small. Dr.
Macdonald Critchley has talked about the punch-drunk syndrome
and admits it is now rare and becoming more so. But this syndrome
is not confined to boxers only and can be seen in people who have
played other rough games but have never boxed. It is not, therefore,
a disease confined to boxers, although it was most commonly seen in

pugilists. But then no sensible person would deny that the repeated hammerings week in week out which some boxers took in the old days were obviously harmful.

Immediate complications do also occur from time to time as Mr. Dickson Wright has told you. Subarachnoid haemorrhage and sub-dural haematoma, and much more rarely frank brain lacerations and tentorial tears and herniations do sometimes happen. They are essentially the province of the neurosurgeon (and perhaps also of the morbid anatomist), and the neurosurgeon will tell you how rare they are. This may be because even the most vigorous punch in boxing, cushioned as it is by the glove and the reactions of the recipient, is seldom so severe as the blow received in the road traffic, industrial, domestic and different type of sporting accident.

There is, of course, a risk of severe intra-cranial injury in boxing —this cannot be denied, but it is relatively slight and can further be reduced by proper control and care. You may feel as I do that in some respects there is at present insufficient care or control, but this is a reason for condemning those responsible rather than the sport itself.

11

Dr. Frank Byrom, M.D., F.R.C.P., F.R.A.C.P.

Department of Neuropathology, Institute of Psychiatry, Maudsley Hospital

(Dr. Byrom presented a lucid account of the types and mechanisms of closed head injury lavishly illustrated by slides.)

The most serious brain injuries in boxing arise in those cases where the force of the blow carries a rotational element. Such rotational injuries set up the maximum amount of turbulence as a result of which the brain swirls about within the skull, and the brain tissue itself is alternately compressed and expanded. This can clearly be shown experimentally. This swirling about will cause the fine vessels between the brain and its coverings to be stretched and torn and will damage the brain tissue itself. No amount of protective headgear short of a really efficient crash helmet which effectively absorbs these forces without transmitting them to the skull will be of any avail, nor will any form of underfloor padding.

Intra-cranial turbulence can be demonstrated even when the force applied to the skull is quite small. It follows, therefore, that any blow to the head in boxing will lead to some degree of damage, and thus as long as the head remains part of the target area the boxing must be regarded as medically unjustifiable.

DISCUSSION

AUDIENCE: It seems clear from what has been said that severe head injuries do indeed occur in boxing, but apart from Mr. Radley Smith no statistics have been quoted. Are any available? Is it known how often these injuries are received? Perhaps Surgeon Commander Watt has some figures on this subject too. May I also ask if there is any information available about the psychiatric sequels of boxing or whether a person is psychologically upset and that makes him take up boxing?

CHAIRMAN: I think we must be agreed that very little is available in the way of real statistical evidence—certainly we must interpret with caution those figures we have already heard.

MR. BILLIMORE: I am not at all happy about this question of possible brain damage, particularly in the case of schoolboys and the younger men. The control of boxing in schools is not all that good and we are worried about the effects of knockouts on schoolboys. We do not know if boxing is likely to impair them mentally and make them less good as scholars and prejudice their futures. I think it has been said elsewhere that there is a high incidence of nervous and mental disorders among university students who box. Could this possibly be a product of brain damage sustained by them when they were younger and still at school?

MR. DICKSON WRIGHT: I am not satisfied that boxing does a schoolboy or a university student a great deal of harm. There are certainly many men who were good and active amateur boxers in their youth who now hold very high and responsible posts in the National Health Service and in other professions. I would not say that they were psychiatric cases.

DR. MACDONALD CRITCHLEY: There is no doubt that mental changes occur in the punch-drunk syndrome, but they appear to be directly associated with distinct cerebral pathology. It seems on the face of it reasonable that only mental changes might occur in some cases, although it might be argued that these represent the earliest stages in the development of the punch-drunk syndrome.

CHAIRMAN: As Dr. Neustatter, who is a psychiatrist, has joined us on the platform, perhaps we should ask for his comment.

DR. W. L. NEUSTATTER: All I can contribute in indicative evidence after thirty years of psychiatry is how little I have come across psychiatric patients who have taken part in boxing. In fact, I think the only boxer I saw had an injury to his leg which he got outside boxing and for which he was claiming compensation. Your chairman did mention the very interesting question of whether boxing has any effect on children as regards mental or educational deterioration. I do not think that I am in a position to answer that without research, but I never had any boy brought to me with that complaint. Another question which has been raised in regard to boys is "does it give them a feeling of confidence to be able to box?" I think it does give confidence, and it is useful to be able to box, but I think it is a very bad thing to force a boy to box who is not inclined to. It seems ridiculous to make people play games if they do not like them, and I say this as a very keen games player myself. I noticed one speaker referred to the high incidence of nervous and mental disorders in university students who box. Is it not the other way round, that unstable people have taken up boxing? I would like to put that question myself. I should have thought the aggressive psychopath and boxing have nothing to do with each other. During the war the aggressive psychopath was quite unfit for commando duties. It was impossible to give him the necessary discipline and exactly the same thing applies to boxing. I should think he would very soon be cured of his desire to box. This was the subject of an article in the *Sunday Times* last week. Somebody expressed the desire to know to what extent boxing is sadistic or masochistic. I cannot for a moment think that any boxer gets sexually excited because he is knocking his opponent about, or himself actually gets sexual pleasure from being hit. These terms are always wrongly used, and really do not apply to boxing. If you take it as meaning pleasure in cruelty or pleasure in being hurt, it seems to me that this is nonsense, as it is in other games. If you ask my personal opinion about the masochistic element in games it does not exist, particularly if you are a bad skier like myself. Similarly in cricket: has Cowdrey a masochistic streak? I do not suppose he enjoyed it when his arm was broken by a bouncer from Hall. Pleasure in boxing, as in all sports, is an artistic one rather than masochistic. If you really like games you are more satisfied in doing something well than in winning, although obviously you want to win as well. At Halton Mental Hospital someone was going through the figures. Since the war there were about 6000 male admissions and in no case had a note been made that there was any kind of dementia or psychological disorder regarding boxing. I was chosen to be neutral and I remain neutral, and I think it does mean something that I have had so little to say. From what I have seen, the effect on the audience may sometimes be undesirable, but is this confined to boxing?

MR. A. J. P. MARTIN: You have, if I may say so, rather challenged me to put the case of the schools' boxing. I wish you had given me due warning, I could have prepared something I am sure which would have been rather illuminating.

Schools have been mentioned on so many occasions over the last two days that I must report to my Association that we have got to consider very carefully whether we should develop schools' boxing or whether, indeed, we should abandon it. I have been rather swamped (and I am sure a number of others have as well) by the medical terms used, but I am still convinced that boxing is good for school-boys. Why does the Association think this of a schoolboy boxing? In the first place it is a natural thing for a boy to fight. Any school-master would know that if you want to assemble a school quickly in the playground all that is necessary is to put two boys in the middle and tell them to start fighting—the school will assemble in a few minutes. It is a natural instinct and we feel we should develop this natural instinct in a form where there can be shown the need for law and order and sensible thinking.

Does boxing adversely affect schoolboys? I would just mention some schoolboy champions. The captain of Cambridge University team two years ago was a former high school boy. We have had a boy from Croydon who became a champion and who also played in the National Youth Orchestra. I was very delighted to meet yester-day a young man who told me that in 1956 he won a Buckingham-shire schools championship and is now doing a third year at Lough-borough College. We do not feel that boxing does any harm—we make very stringent rules and take stringent precautions. We instruct our referees most thoroughly that as soon as a boy seems to be having the worst of it, the bout is to be stopped immediately. We do not have the count; there is no such thing as a schoolboy being counted out. We do not wear bandages; we do not feel it is necessary for a schoolboy. We carry out various experiments. For example, we are holding a series of contests in which the boys will be judged not so much from the attacking point of view but from the skills. We are also going to experiment by trying the use of the pneumatic glove. I would also recommend that we try the headgear, but a boy does not like to dress up too much. If he goes into the ring, he is not forced to box although some boxing instruction may come as part of a normal P.E. lesson. Most boxing takes place after school. No boy is so foolish as to go into the ring and stand waiting for his opponent to hit him—there is just as much joy in defending, in countering well, as in attack. The thing that does concern me and concerns my Association is that in so many cases there is no correct instruction given in schools. We do not like to affiliate a school unless there is a teacher capable and knowledgeable in instructing. So many injuries come from the incorrect delivery of blows and from not knowing the correct movements. I would throw the blame for this on the training colleges and on the organizers of Physical Education. If people would allow us to show what we have done about the good parts of boxing, I am sure it would help to improve instruction in training colleges and also convince some of the educational organizers that there is some good in the sport. We ask for restrictions on the number of bouts that a boy can box and also we ask for the fights to be time spaced. Two weights of glove are used according to the various classes. In championships we give a weight allowance which is apportioned over the time a boy takes through the various stages. He is not allowed to concede more than one year or 5 lb in weight for ordinary school contests and more than one year or 7 lb for championships. We like a boy to box at his natural weight. We object to the skipping and the sweating and we do insist that each boy has his own beaker and his own sponge.

I mentioned experiments such as that of using a four-rope ring. We have dealt with gum-shields and I am certain that if we could get into the training colleges the need to give boys the skills of boxing, it would have an influence in the schools and obviously on the A.B.A. and, although I am not personally interested, on the professionals. There is no more danger to young people in this sport which is nowadays so well controlled and supervised both medically and otherwise than in any other field of sport.

Mr. W. R. CAMPBELL: I come from a training college and I did not come to answer the points raised by the previous speaker. I would like to say that we are free in training colleges to a considerable extent to choose to teach those things which we think are of most advantage. In my college boxing ranks very low among the many other things which Physical Education has to offer and is therefore not part of the curriculum. Speaking about the recent interview on television following the fight between Walker and Prescott, I was very impressed by the things Prescott said when he was asked what he thought of the big punching of Walker. The punches which worried him were not the ones which rendered him unconscious; the punches which were the worst were the hard ones which were not hard enough to render him insensible. I wonder if the boxer who is knocked out is indeed the fortunate one rather than the one who remains on his feet. A rain of blows is much more accumulatively damaging than one knockout punch. I think that there should be compulsory medical examination of boxers after technical knockouts as well as stricter discipline of coaches, boxers and referees.

SURGEON COMMANDER WATT, R.N.: Since my statistics have been quoted I should mention that I brought them up in connection with a regional injury, namely hand injuries, and they were out-patient attendances to which I was referring. I think that this illustrates one of the many imponderables in this problem. Someone has asked, for instance, whether these sailors had been trained properly. The majority of sailors do get some training in boxing, but it might be equally argued that because they had been taught that this was the manly way to settle an argument, this is how they do it and there might have been less injuries as a result of the fight on shore had not that attitude of mind been inculcated at an early age. I quoted these figures yesterday because of the calls for statistics and they were out-patient injuries in hand cases. Here are some of our statistics for in-patient cases.

In the R.N. Hospital in Haslar in 1962 we had a total of 248 admissions as a result of sports injuries. Analysis shows that these 248 people had a total of 5708 days in hospital, an average of 23 days to every patient and a total days disability of 15,701. We could perhaps compare organized soccer, in which we had 114 cases, with organized boxing in which we only had 11. The boxers' hospital days were an average of 9 to every patient and their total disability 17 days to every patient as opposed to non-organized boxing (which really ought not to be allowed, but does happen). There we find the hospital days were 27 to 1 as compared with 9 to 1—total days disability 40 to every patient as opposed to 17 to every patient in the controlled and organized games. Do these statistics prove that boxing is a safe sport? Certainly we have very few cases, but I think it has to be remembered that, in the Portsmouth Command at least, those taking part in boxing are less than one half of 1 per cent of the personnel in the Command, which is an infinitesimally smaller number than those taking part in soccer or rugby. We can compare the death rates of various types of sports, and sailing and swimming had a higher death rate than any other. We might compare the head injury rate—rugby football had a higher head injury rate. We could take, for instance, the fact that in 1964 an electroencephalogram was taken on all boxers and that did not reveal anything significant, only succeeding in picking up a single case of epilepsy which was not very conclusive. It is very difficult to reach any firm conclusion about the evidence that is presented. For instance, even the medical evidence is prejudiced. Yesterday somebody quoted Mr. Pennybacker in the B.M.A. meeting this year who saw more head injuries as a result of riding rather than boxing. But Mr. Pennybacker also said that he was actually in a riding county where he would expect to find head injuries as a result of riding. It was pointed out that Mr. Pennybacker had also said that we must regard every incident of unconsciousness as causing the death of a certain number of neurones. If there is any evidence, it is that the cumulative effect can only result in the death of a number of neurones. Although this punch-drunk syndrome has been glossed over by some it seems it may have a real significance. It is important to know whether we ought to advise the parents of promising youngsters that they ought not to take up boxing. Let me show you how valueless all these statistics are that I have quoted. I was talking to a friend of mine who said that I might be interested to hear of a psychiatric case in an adjacent Naval Hospital. It was the story of a young man of 32, an able seaman who had been in 1959 a Fleet champion and in 1960 was knocked out for the fifteenth time. He then began to be absent over leave, he became inefficient at his job and unsatisfactory in his home. His wife said he had previously been an affectionate husband, reliable and capable, with concern for money matters. He had become disinterested, got into debt and trouble and his work had fallen off. As a result of this he was ultimately referred to a neuro-psychiatrist and his syndrome was typical of that described today by Dr. Macdonald Critchley. Here is an example in 1962 which would have been missed in this group of statistics but for a casual conversation in the Mess with some colleagues. It does show that if we are going to come to any logical conclusion about it, we have to say that there are many imponderables and that though the actual physical injuries are minimal in boxing as compared with certain other sports, there is a very real danger that the odd individual may sustain some permanent neurological damage.

SURGEON CAPTAIN C. B. NICHOLSON: There are very few injuries that we get in school boxing. We find that the pattern of hand and finger injuries does not quite follow what we heard yesterday. I only remember one or two Bennett's fractures in five years. Possibly boxers do break their fingers and put their thumbs out of alignment, but this may be a question of training or what glove is used. Could we reduce these injuries which are not in the pattern of normal hand and wrist injuries by better training or by a different form of glove? I would just like to support the previous speaker about the care that is taken in the ring. There is no actual looking for knockouts—every bout is stopped if there is any danger of that at all. Boys are always compared carefully for weight, age and height and in fact some of the best boxers do not get a bout at all because they are too good for the opposition. I see very few unconscious cases, I think a knockout in schoolboy boxing hardly exists, and actual unconsciousness does not seem to occur, or only very seldom. It is very occasionally that I feel it is necessary to have somebody under observation after boxing, but much more so after rugby football.

MR. A. McDOUGALL: I have read Dr. Critchley's papers and, being a doctor and having a family of my own, it is encumbent on me to ensure that if the pathological conditions he describes do happen, I must speak against boxing. Since 1932 I have been associated with university boxing—I have boxed for my university and I have been knocked out, but I do not think that I have suffered any material damage on that score. As Mr. Dickson Wright has said, the many ex-boxers who now hold important positions in the National Health Service shows that they have not suffered very great brain damage. I was surprised to hear about nervous instability and mental disorders in university students. Since my association with university boxing in 1932 until the present day, I have not had any student who has suffered any nervous instability or mental upset. This summer, my son, who is a medical student, spent three months abroad with a former opponent of mine in the ring who is now Dean of a foreign medical school, so it surprised me to hear all this about nervous instability. We have got to look at this thing logically and weigh the pros and cons. If I am convinced when I leave here that boxing will have a permanent effect on the mental capacity of any of my students, then I will have it banned at the university. On Friday next week my university will box Liverpool University and I am hoping that Dick McTaggart will give an exhibition. Here is a boy who has fought close on 400 fights—there are few of us who have not seen McTaggart on television, and if anyone doubts his mental capacity, I would invite them to play him at cards. With regard to punch-drunkenness, I do not deny that it exists, but I have only seen it in professional boxers who have fought for many, many years under conditions that would not be tolerated nowadays, and the people concerned are all of the older age group.

DR. FRANK BYROM: With regard to the question of knocks on the head short of unconsciousness, clearly they can do damage. Whether they do more or less damage than a straight knockout is simply a matter of guesswork. The only point I would like to make is that I do not know why it is necessary for Mr. Doggart and others to demonstrate that boxing damages the brain; surely it is the function of the doctors connected with boxing. If they had demonstrated that it does not, there would not be this fall-off in boxing, nor would there be this inquiry going on at the College of Physicians.

DR. MCDONALD CRITCHLEY: I have seen a state very like mild punch-drunkenness in a footballer once. He had been knocked out many times on the rugger field. Is punch-drunkenness a disappearing disease? The conditions under which people used to box are quite different from the conditions under which professional boxers are operating now, and it may well be that we shall see fewer and fewer of these punch-drunken cases but we cannot be sure. We are still seeing cases in their thirties. We are only in the stage of fact finding. Dr. Blonstein and I both remember the same amateur boxers who were punch-drunk and three other amateurs who may well be. Who were these youngsters that were killed in the ring? They were cases which did not occur in this country, but they have been published. If a professional does not die one cannot see pinpoint haemorrhages at that stage. There have been one or two cases of boxers who have died from something else and pinpoint haemorrhages have been demonstrated with the greatest of ease.

Too much discussion has been emotionally charged today as to whether boxing is a bad thing or a good thing. We are still in the stage of collecting facts. Mr. Campbell raised the point, is it worse to be knocked out or to be knocked out on your feet? I am inclined to think that an accumulation of what one calls a groggy state is probably worse than, or as bad as, an accumulation of complete knockouts.

CHAIRMAN: I am inclined to support Dr. McDonald Critchley that there is an enormous lot more to learn. We know these things happen but it is manifestly clear that they are rare in boxing as compared with motor-cycling and many other activities. Here is a final point. If we do not approve of boxing, how strong is our obligation to interfere and to prevent?

SESSION V

MEDICAL CARE OF THE BOXER

Chairman

SIR ARTHUR PORRITT, Bt., K.C.M.G., K.C.V.O., C.B.E., F.R.C.S.
Chairman, British Association of Sport and Medicine

12

Lt.-Col. J. W. Graham, L.M.S.S.A.

Chairman, Medical Sub-Committee, British Boxing Board of Control
President, Medical Commission, European Boxing Union

Up to the 1920's the only time a boxer came under medical care was after an injury. He was then treated by his own doctor or in hospital. With the formation, in 1929, of the British Boxing Board of Control, two official medical officers were appointed, one in London and one in the north.

The chief duty of the medical officers appointed was to examine boxers on behalf of the Board if, for example, a championship was involved and a boxer was said to be unfit. However, regulations were soon made that boxers must be medically examined before a contest and a medical officer should be in attendance to attend to injured boxers.

The medical implications of boxing were rarely considered by boxers, managers, promoters and, indeed, the public, and the medical aspects received scant consideration from the profession. A boxer, no matter what his injury, was expected to carry on fighting as long as he could lift himself off the ring floor. There was a widely held belief that there is a particular spot on the jaw a blow on which, if hard enough, produces immediate insensibility. Recovery occurred as from normal sleep and the recipient of the blow was none the worse for it. This view was popularized by writers of all kinds—and seemed to be confirmed by the fact that in most cases a knocked-out boxer apparently recovered completely within a very short time.

Followers of the sport, however, realized that a boxer who suffered frequent knockouts might become punch-drunk. This was regarded as a hazard of the sport and occurred to boxers who preferred to fight rather than box and who were content, in their contests, to exchange blow for blow rather than make efforts to defend themselves.

With regard to the physical injuries of boxers there is no point in going into the superstitious and sometimes barbaric methods of prevention and treatment favoured by many managers and trainers. Under the Board of Control, by 1939 boxers had been advised to give up these methods and, in the case of injuries, to take and act on medical advice.

During World War II most of the stewards were scattered in the various services as, indeed, were most of the boxers, trainers and managers. Hundreds of thousands of contests took place at all levels in the various Services under the medical charge of Service doctors whose sole concern was to see that contestants were comparatively fit before boxing and to treat them afterwards if they needed it.

With the end of the war, the Board of Control became firmly established as the controlling body of professional boxing in Britain. By their constitution, however, they were not an autocratic body as, for example, the Jockey Club, and before any new regulations governing boxing became operative they had to be passed by a majority of the members. As all the members, with the exception of the stewards, were financially interested in the sport, much-needed reforms in the regulations governing the sport often took longer to become operative than they should. This applied to certain suggestions for a stricter medical control.

However, the Board decided that stricter control was needed with the result that in each of the eight areas of the Board an honorary medical officer and sufficient deputy medical officers to cope with the work in the area were appointed. A Medical Committee of the Board was formed consisting of chairman, the area medical officers, their deputies and any stewards who were medically qualified.

In spite of the anxiety of the Board and its willingness to implement recommendations made by the Medical Committee, matters did not always move as quickly as possible. One of the first snags came from a sub-committee of the British Medical Association who wanted to know who was going to pay for the very comprehensive initial medical examination which was compared with that required by a life insurance company for a considerable amount. This difficulty and others were overcome and the Medical Committee made a number of recommendations to the Board which implemented them. Among these were a series of compulsory medical examinations. Briefly—these were before a licence was granted; on the annual renewal of a licence; before and after contests and before resuming boxing one month after having been knocked out in a contest.

The minimum age of boxers and the number of rounds and number of contests to be engaged in by young boxers was also defined. This at first met with some opposition as it was felt by many managers that each boxer should be treated as an individual. The Medical Committee of the Board, however, considered that no boxer should be allowed to box more than one contest of even three or four rounds within four clear days of his last contest or six clear days for chief contests and this became a regulation.

The present weight of the gloves is 6 oz. The return of the 4 oz glove has been seriously recommended by informed medical opinion as being less likely to cause brain damage. It was, however, rejected by the Medical Committee because of the severe facial damage which could result. The 8 oz glove was rejected for the average boxer as more likely to cause brain damage because of the wider diffusion of the force of a blow and what has been described as the thudding effect of the heavier weight.

Although bandages were introduced primarily to protect the hands it was found in practice that many boxers, by building the bandages and tapes over the knuckles, were using them as weapons of offence particularly inside "broken gloves". Regulations governing the amount of bandage permitted and the method of application of the bandages have been introduced to prevent this, and the breaking of gloves is strictly prohibited.

It was considered important to adopt minimum standards of visual acuity which was done after consultation with a number of ophthalmic surgeons. Myopes are refused a licence as it is thought that they are more prone to suffer from a detached retina.

All manner of substances, from spiders' webs to solutions of cowdung or strong coagulating concoctions of iron, tannin and even nitric acid, were in common use as haemostatics. Many other substances have been considered by the Medical Committee, but rejected for various reasons, and the only one permitted nowadays is 1 in 1000 adrenalin solution. Some American boxers use adrenalin in an ointment base.

Competent surgeons suggested that cuts round the eye could be sutured during the inter-round intervals. This idea was rejected out of hand, and managers, seconds and referees now know that if bleeding cannot be controlled by adrenalin the contest must be stopped.

Formerly, ring floors were covered by canvas with a varying

thickness of felt underneath. Post-mortem reports on a number of boxers who received fatal injuries showed that the actual cause of death was ruptured pial vein, due in some cases to a boxer striking the back of his head with considerable force on an inadequately protected ring floor. After the introduction of a protective matting in the United States, the New York State Athletic Commission reported that its introduction was the biggest factor in reducing fatalities from fourteen in one year to none in the next.

Our own Government Road Research Laboratory carried out experiments to find the ideal shock-absorbing substance for lining crash helmets. The one with the highest shock-absorbing capacity was unsuitable for ring matting as it is fragile and unstable under temperature changes. A satisfactory matting, however, made from nitrogen-expanded rubber, has been developed and the use of this had now been made compulsory by the Board. The essential difference between this substance and others which are unsuitable, such as sponge rubber, is that it is of a closed cell construction. It does not in any way impede the movements of a boxer.

The Board issue precise instructions as to how an unconscious boxer is to be handled. Aromatic ammonia or any other form of stimulant is most expressly forbidden.

Experienced medical officers are not always available up and down the country to officiate at tournaments. The combined experience of the medical committee of the Board is very considerable and they issue instructions covering the various matters to all tournament medical officers.

For those who are not familiar with the technique of "drying-out", it consists of the total deprivation of fluid for anything up to three full days before a boxer is weighed in. This results in considerable weight reduction. The evils arising from this and other abnormal methods of weight reduction have been explained to boxers and managers, and disciplinary action is taken by the Board against boxers or managers found using them.

Some controlling bodies have made a regulation which says that after a knockdown a boxer must take a compulsory rest of 8 seconds before resuming boxing. On the face of it this appears to be a sensible regulation in that in some cases it enables a boxer to recover completely before resuming boxing. The medical committee of the Board, however, do not agree. Under it, a contest may continue when, in the interest of the boxer, it should be stopped. Referees are instructed that under no circumstances must they allow a boxer to be struck by his opponent unless he is in a position to defend himself. If a boxer gets to his feet after a count of four, dazed, and is not then in a position to defend himself, the contest should be stopped. If he is given another 4 seconds in which to place himself in a defensive position he is, in many cases, very likely to receive a further damaging blow or blows.

All boxing must stand or fall on the question as to whether the punch-drunk syndrome can be prevented. It is the view of myself and my committee that it can, and indeed it no longer occurs in professional boxing under the British Boxing Board of Control, so that nowadays very few medical men have ever seen a case.

Fourteen years ago the late Professor Kennedy, then Honorary Medical Officer to the A.B.A., called a conference of medical officers associated with European Amateur Boxing in Copenhagen to discuss the punch-drunk syndrome. I attended, by invitation, as the representative of the British Boxing Board of Control. It was very evident that although we all recognized the syndrome, none of us knew much about it. When the Medical Committee was first formed it was found that the medical literature on the punch-drunk syndrome was almost non-existent. Inquiries from the "Any Questions" column of the *British Medical Journal* as to the early signs and symptoms of the syndrome were completely unproductive. The Editor of the *Journal* went to a very considerable amount of trouble to try to obtain some information on the subject, but very little was available. One of my colleagues may go further into what we now think are the early signs of the syndrome and its prognosis. I will be content with indicating what the Medical Committee have done and are doing to prevent it occurring. Before doing this, however, one or two observations. None of the eight post-mortem reports in my possession on boxers who have been fatally injured in the ring mention previous brain damage except to say that there was no evidence of any.

Dr. Kaplin, a neurosurgeon on the staff of the New York State Hospital, after three years' investigation of boxers and contests at the ringside involving some thousands of electro-encephalograms and some miles of slow-motion film taken at the ringside and paid for by the State of New York, assured me personally that, in his opinion, there is no such condition. I do not agree with him, but I am inclined to think that the condition does not occur in a normally stable nervous system. It must not be forgotten that there are many boxers alive today who boxed under the pre-medical control regulations who are physically and mentally better off than the majority of people of their age. With very few exceptions no new cases of the syndrome have been observed in professional boxing in this country for the last twelve years. Exceptions are due to boxing abroad or in booths.

The precise pathology of encephalopathy is unknown. Patechial haemorrhages in the cortex or other parts of the brain with subsequent fibrosis is an old theory, but as far as I know has never been demonstrated. It is worthy of note that in one case where we had withdrawn a boxer's licence because he was showing what we consider to be the early signs of encephalopathy, the boxer provided certificates from eminent neurologists saying that he was fit to continue boxing.

Under the constitution of the Board, a boxer is entitled to appeal against a decision of the administrative stewards to the stewards of appeal. This, this boxer did and an eminent neurologist appeared before the stewards of appeal as a witness on behalf of the boxer. The stewards of appeal, however, upheld the views of the Medical Committee of the Board and the licence was not renewed. Other boxers have produced similar certificates after a period of rest, but we consider that if a boxer has once shown signs of encephalopathy his licence should not be renewed, and it is not renewed.

In most cases when a boxer is advised by the Board's representative to give up boxing he does so without demur, but in some cases he goes abroad to certain States in America or elsewhere and resumes boxing there. Again, some go into booths which are not under the jurisdiction of the Board, whilst others continue to box in gyms or hire themselves out abroad as sparring partners. The Board now has a liaison with most of the controlling bodies throughout the world to prevent this.

Comparatively few boxers are rendered immediately completely unconscious in the ring. They become temporarily dazed and are not able to co-ordinate movements. In these cases the contest should be immediately stopped by the referee who also has strict instructions to stop a contest where one boxer is obviously outclassed. The referee must always stop a contest if one of the boxers is unable to defend himself. Before resuming boxing after a knockout a boxer must be free from signs and symptoms of any description.

Other methods of prevention are to stop boxers who are temporarily or permanently suspended from boxing in gyms. Professional boxers are prevented from boxing too often and great care is taken to see that they are never overmatched. No professional boxer can box abroad without the permission of the Board who must know and approve the opponent. This we consider to be very important. Even though a man is in every way physically fit, unless there are special circumstances such as a good amateur record, boxers over the age of twenty-six would not be given a licence.

We believe that if a boxer stops boxing if and when he shows what we believe are the early signs of likely damage he will recover completely. In any event we know that he will show no signs or have any symptoms after a very short time. To say, as has been said, that he will show signs later on is, in our opinion, unjustifiable speculation. The Board stops a boxer as soon as the earliest signs are apparent to the experienced observer and as a result we believe the punch-drunk syndrome has been eliminated.

With the introduction of the safety mat, limitation of the amount of tape and bandages to be used, precautions against overmatching, etc., and instructions already given to referees we hope that fatal accidents have been eliminated. In any case they have certainly been reduced to a very small number in proportion to any other sport.

Boxing is already safer than most other sports. Those who wish to box are entitled to do so. They are entitled to see and enjoy professional boxing which is boxing at its best just as much as others are entitled to watch professional football, golf or any other sport.

I am often asked by virtue of the position which I am proud to hold in the British Boxing Board of Control whether boys should be allowed to box. My answer is invariably the same. Any boy who wishes to box should be encouraged to do so under supervision, but anybody that makes a boy box who does not want to should himself be put in the ring with Sonny Liston.

13

Dr. J. L. Blonstein, M.R.C.S., L.R.C.P., D.I.H.

Honorary Medical Officer, Amateur Boxing Association
General Secretary, World Medical Commission, A.I.B.A.

When a boy joins an Amateur Boxing Club, his medical welfare starts straight away. He is immediately given a complete medical examination either by the club's medical officer or, in London, by a member of the Medical Panel consisting of over 100 doctors who give their services free. If there is any suspicion of chest or cardiac disease or if there is a suspicious family history, the boy is given a chest X-ray or an electrocardiogram. We have found boys with heart disease playing football and swimming. One boy had a loud systolic murmur and on investigation was found to have a congenital form of heart disease and yet he was playing football. If this boy had been allowed to box without a previous examination, serious consequences might have followed. We have fixed eye standards, and any boy who has five diopters of myopia or more is definitely banned from boxing. We do not accept boys with squint. In all doubtful cases the boxer is referred to a consultant for his opinion.

We introduced this scheme in London ten years ago and it is now being followed all over the British Isles. We are now considering issuing a certificate annually stating that the boy has not had any serious illness or accident during the previous year. This he will have to obtain from his own medical officer and this in addition to the fact that he is examined every time he presents himself to box in a contest.

With reference to eyes we have now introduced a new rule whereby a boxer must produce a certificate from an ophthalmic practitioner once every three years, stating that his eyesight has not deteriorated.

The boxer has a medical card recording any injuries and the period the boxer is to stay off, so that when a boxer presents himself for a subsequent contest the medical officer who examines him can see at a glance what previous injuries he has received and can judge if the boy has sufficiently recovered. It is also the duty of the official in charge of the tournament to see that the boxer's injuries are recorded on his card. A medical officer is present during the contests and attends to minor injuries, and it is compulsory for an authorized first-aid box to be supplied by the organizing club. The more serious injuries are, of course, sent to hospital.

To give you examples of the periods off boxing, if a boy sustains a cut in the region of the eye (when I say a cut I mean a laceration whereby the thickness of the skin is split) he is put off for at least four weeks, and for a boy who is knocked out (and when I talk about a knockout I mean a boy who has lost consciousness for any period of time) the minimum period he is put off boxing and training is four weeks.

Before I come to the question of head injuries and how we deal with them, perhaps I might say something about a boxer going down as a result of a blow to the solar plexus. He may go down and be counted out but yet he remains completely conscious throughout this time, and we have seen no permanent ill effects as a result of a knockout by a blow to the solar plexus. Following a knockout as a result of a blow to the head (and again my definition of a knockout is when a boxer becomes unconscious as a result of a blow) most boxers regain consciousness by the count of ten and are able to walk to their corners unassisted. In my experience, the majority are able to get up comfortably by the count of seven. If consciousness has not been regained by the end of the count the boxer is allowed to recover on the floor of the ring. His head is supported and turned to one side, making sure that there is a good airway. If he remains unconscious for any length of time he is removed from the ring on a stretcher and sent to hospital for observation. If there is any antegrade, or post-traumatic amnesia, even without loss of consciousness, this is treated as concussion and the patient admitted to hospital. In our statistics we find that there are about 1 per cent of knockouts in the course of tournaments, and for a boxer to become dazed by a head blow more than once in a bout is extremely rare. *En passant*, let us compare this with what happens at football where you see a footballer becoming unconscious on the field as a result of a kick or some other injury. He is given the wet-sponge treatment and is immediately allowed to go on playing. I think, as far as boxing goes, we do look after the participants very much better.

Now I want to say just a few words about the EEG—the electro-encephalogram which measures the brain waves. These are not absolutely pathognomonic, that is to say, you cannot make a definite diagnosis by looking at a tracing and you cannot say that because a tracing is negative there has been no injury. But taking the EEG with other investigations and clinical signs one can form a diagnosis. Dr. Edwin Clark of the Post Graduate Hospital of Medicine at Hammersmith and I have examined the EEGs of some seventy-eight boys who have been knocked out and we did not find any abnormal changes—as I see it this may not be pathognomic but it rather suggests that boys who have been knocked out do not necessarily suffer any permanent damage. We are constantly making trials and studies on amateur boxers and we examined 100 young amateur boxers before boxing—their ages were between 17 and 27 with a majority between 19 and 20, followed by the 22–23 group. All had a previous complete medical examination before boxing. The record-ing apparatus was a portable echo with eight leads which was placed in a room communicating directly with the hall in which the boxing took place. In order to note the degree of injuries and their con-sequences the progress of the bouts was followed. On leaving the ring, the boxer who had been injured was immediately taken to the examination room. Two assistants facilitated the rapid preparation of the subjects. Out of 100 boxers who had had a previous systematic EEG we were able to examine fifty-two boxers in 4–6 minutes after they had left the ring. What I want to point out is the fact that in these tracings young boys have slow posterior waves in their EEGs and this is taken by some investigators (particularly Larson in America) as signs of brain damage. He found these changes in young boxers and suggested that they were caused by damage to the brain as a result of boxing. But I can show you that in 48 per cent of the cases that we examined we found the slow posterior waves in normal boys who had not boxed.

The conclusions we came to after a series of 100 cases was that alterations observed after boxing are not pathological. The changes are functional or physiological. EEG tracings are greatly disturbed after injuries, but the alterations do not persist after 4–6 minutes even when there has been loss of consciousness for more than 10 seconds. But the important thing that one learns from this study is that when evaluating the results of EEG examinations, account must be taken of the possibility of the existence of significant posterior slow waves prior to the trauma, and they must not be interpreted as a manifestation of recently acquired disturbance.

Let us now consider what steps are taken in amateur boxing to reduce the number of injuries. Juniors under the age of 15 only box three 1½-minute rounds. Those boys between 15 and 16 box two of 1½ minutes, and one of 2 minutes, and those between the ages of 16 and 17 box three 2-minute rounds. Seniors, of course, box three 3-minute rounds. Not only are the boys matched in competitions regarding their experience and their accomplishments, but they also match for weight and age naturally. No junior may concede more than 5 lb in weight or more than 12 months in age. Looking at a referee's powers from the medical point of view they have strict instructions to stop a bout if a boy receives a cut or a deep abrasion or if a boxer is obviously outclassed, if he is knocked down and appears dazed on rising, or if he cannot defend himself.

We have in amateur boxing the compulsory eight count. If a boy is knocked down as a result of a blow, even if he gets up at two or three, he must take a rest of 8 seconds. We feel it gives him a chance to pull himself together again. The boy may even be given a stand-up count, that is to say he need not necessarily be down. If he appears dazed to the referee, then he is given a count of 8 seconds. Another important rule we have introduced is that the boxer can no longer be saved by the bell. In the past you may have seen a boxer lying unconscious in the ring at the end of a round, to be then carried or assisted to his corner, revived, and pushed back into the ring only to receive another blow and become unconscious again. If a boxer is down at the end of a round the bell does not sound, the count goes on, and if he cannot be up at the count of ten then he is counted out. Of course, this does not happen at the end of the third round. So you will no longer have the spectacle in amateur boxing of an unconscious boxer being taken back to his corner and expected to box on again.

The referee has the power to disqualify a boxer for butting, using the elbow, rabbit punches, kidney punches, wrestling, ducking below the belt when the head may strike the opponent's abdomen or for low punches.

The gloves must weigh at least 8 oz—that is for seniors; those for juniors weighing 6½ stone or under have 6 oz gloves, and juniors over the weight of 6½ stone have 8 oz gloves. The gloves must be well padded so as to soften and spread the blow, and are laceless to prevent lacerations. It may interest you to know that we have been experimenting with a pneumatic glove and, as you have probably heard, the Schools Boxing Association is going to give them a trial this season. This glove consists of a very fine leather glove with a plastic bladder inside. This bladder is pumped up with an ordinary bicycle pump. It reduces the force of the blow by just under 50 per cent. The hand is made into the shape of the fist and is inserted in that position. There is no compartment for the thumb (and as you heard from the speakers on hand injuries the thumb is the digit most often injured in boxing) and it is well protected inside this glove. The whole of the fist is surrounded with a pad of air. As it cuts down the force of the blow by 50 per cent we hope to reduce the number of head injuries. At the same time, the fine soft leather of the glove will also, we hope, diminish the number of cuts. We are also experimenting with a pneumatic headgear. As you know, most boxers, both amateur and professional, use headgear for training and, speaking personally, I see no reason why headgear should not be worn in the ring for contests. The American Armed Forces have already adopted headgear and it is obvious that they have reduced the number of head injuries considerably. They use a headgear with sorbo rubber, and we have experimented with a pneumatic one, again filled with air. It is very simple and very light and, again, we hope the schools will try it out. I believe Major Webb of the Army Boxing Association would like to try the gloves and headgear for Army boxers, and we are going to let him have a set. This headgear is very simple, very light and it protects the two most important parts—the front of the head and the back of the head. As has been stated (and it is our experience) most of the damage to the head is caused by the boxer falling with his occiput on to the floor of the ring.

As you heard, amateur boxers now have Velpo bandages to protect their metacarpals, and they are advised to wear mouth-pieces made of resilient material which they have specially fitted to their own measurements. This, of course, protects the teeth and lips, and also has another important function. It reduces the force of the blow which is transmitted from the lower jaw to the upper jaw and then to the brain. Many people do not know about the importance of the gum-shield.

As I said, many of the injuries to the head are caused by the occiput striking the floor of the ring, and the Amateur Boxing Association has provided the sorbo rubber or felt floor cover which is five-eighths of an inch thick. We cannot have it any thicker because it would interfere with the footwork of the boxer. Recently we have been experimenting with a new plastic material which the Finns are using and which I think is even superior to the sorbo, and I hope to see it introduced into amateur rings.

We encourage the boys to wear jock-straps, and the International Amateur body have made the wearing of cups compulsory.

We are constantly making studies on amateur boxers and seeing what we can do to improve their welfare. As most of you know, three years ago we introduced the use of streptokinase and strepto-dornase in the treatment of bruises and haematomas, and over the years we have formed an impression that they have been useful and, in fact, now many amateur boxers will not take part in a contest unless these tablets are available.

This, of course, is only one way in which we assist the amateur boxer. Not only do we look after the boxer from his actual boxing point of view, but the clubs make a point of looking into the home life of the boxer. We try to see that they get decent jobs, we often go to their homes and speak to their parents, and many a mother has to be given advice on feeding these boys.

Today we heard many speakers ask about the possible mental deterioration of boy boxers, and it may interest you to know that over the last $3\frac{1}{2}$ years we have been carrying out a study on 200 schoolboys, half of whom box and half of whom do not. These are boys who are between the ages of 11 and 15. We take their I.Q.s and do aptitude tests every six months and also follow up their scholastic attainments and see what jobs they take on leaving school. We have not completed this study because it is going to take five years to complete, but, so far, we can find no significant differences between the boxers and the non-boxers. Their scholastic attainments are fairly equal and just as many boxers take up and enter professions. One boy, who has had over 200 bouts as an amateur, won an open scholarship to Queen's College, Cambridge, so obviously his 200 bouts did not affect his cerebrum very much. We feel that amateur boxing is a useful and justifiable sport providing it is properly controlled.

DISCUSSION

REV. HARRIS: I would like to say, unless there should be any misunderstanding, that the only two things I have never done in the boxing world are to box or to teach boxing. I came into boxing thirty years ago when I had taken a part-time job as a club leader in order to get free board and lodging. There I met the boxing section of the club and two old boys who were shortly afterwards national champions. I found them exceedingly pleasant people indeed and I began to take an interest in their activities. They wanted to make the club into an affiliated club and asked me if I would do the administrative work. It was most noticeable what extremely pleasant boys and young men formed this section.

At Hoxton I discovered the fact that the very limited number of boys who like boxing were benefiting greatly by taking part in it. There was a boy who later became a junior champion. We had only just started a club, and the local headmaster was prejudiced against boxing. I asked him to come and see for himself. He said he could not come but would send his senior master and senior members of the staff. There they saw this young boy defeat a more experienced boxer. The senior master remarked afterwards that if I had told him before that the boy could do that he would never have believed me. He told me that if he spoke roughly to him in class he burst into tears and that he never played games. That boy never burst into tears again, took up team games and became perfectly normal. I do not know what it is that boxing does to boys that need that sort of help. James Wyatt, one of my predecessors in the chair of the A.B.A., thought that it was the absolute isolation of the boxer meeting somebody of the same weight, same age, and so on, when any mistake on his part might mean him losing, that gave him self-respect and self-confidence. This is my opinion also.

As I have gone through life I have been involved with boxing and now meeting young men who have been through the boxing clubs, the more I see of them the less do I regret the time I have given to the sport. I have no use for boxing unless it is properly controlled and properly taught. Having a bash is pernicious. Where boxing is properly taught and the boys properly trained I think it gives a degree of self-confidence and self-control to those boys (who are mostly inoffensive in their manner) and does an immeasurable amount of good. This has been my experience in over thirty years.

Recently there has been much criticism of boxing, but much of it has been uninformed. For example, in my area a boy died after a bout. I went to the inquest and it came out that this boy, who had only just started boxing and who did not appear to have been hit hard either by the glove or by the floor, had been to his family doctor and told him that when hit by anything he got a pain in the head. The doctor said: "I cannot explain it but you had better not do any boxing." Three days later the boy was carefully examined by an A.B.A. doctor and asked if there was anything wrong with him— he said there was nothing wrong with him at all—he lied to the A.B.A. It was asked at the inquest whether that boy might just as well have died as a result of tripping and hitting his head. It was agreed that it was. But that death goes down as a death as a result of boxing. I am not impressed by a lot of this sort of criticism.

If two boys box each other in a ring and a month later you meet them at another tournament you will find them meeting as friends and cheering one another on. I always distrust the saying that a child is mentally defective because as a baby he was dropped, and the same sort of thing is said sometimes of boxers. A lot of the things that are alleged against amateur boxing can happen anywhere. It seems that the whole world is garnered for evidence on damage after boxing. If damage in many other things was covered in the same way the figures would be astronomical. When a distinguished medical man says something in favour of boxing it is frequently not mentioned. And there are those who appear to me to go right outside the subject of their expert knowledge. I heard that an ophthalmic surgeon had been talking here and had said that boxing was a degrading occupation. I would just as soon hear the opinion of a plumber on that. It seems that when people dislike something like boxing they unconsciously find every reason for denouncing what they dislike. I have two boys and a foster child, none taking up boxing. If they had wished to take up boxing I should have been completely delighted and pleased, and thought it would have been a very good thing for them.

It is clear to a fair-minded person that amateur boxing has elements of danger which are slight compared with a great many other sports.

In my opinion, these are greatly outweighed by the great advantages to the very limited section of the juvenile population who like it and do it because they like it. If I had not believed that I would not have had anything to do with boxing.

COLONEL RUSSELL (President of the International A.B.A.): I am president of an Association to which over 100 nations belong. All these nations have varying numbers of boxers, but added together they must amount, and they do amount, to millions. If boxing is a wrongful and pernicious sport, then I must be the most guilty man in the world. On the contrary, I sleep soundly because in every country we have the help, guidance, advice and protection of medical men. That is our safeguard and our standard. All those devoted men with no payment and with no reward except their interest in what they believe to be a healthful and character-building sport, are concerned in research and observation as to any steps that should and can be taken to protect the young boxers for whom they are responsible, and I would like at this medical meeting to express our thanks on behalf of all these millions of young men for what the doctors do for us. I would like to say one word to those of the medical profession who criticize the sport, because I know that they do it with great sincerity and for reasons which they believe are justified from their great medical experience. Their view is that boxing should be stopped. I do not think that this will happen in our time and not in a sport that is so widespread throughout the world and appeals to the natural instincts of man. It is man's natural instinct to put up his fists, and we teach him to do so in a disciplined and controlled way. If these critics would realize that the sport will go on and instead of saying it must be stopped they would say: "Well, we have these criticisms to make but we will from our knowledge and experience give to you our advice and help as to how to reduce these objections and to co-operate with these other doctors", I consider that the whole medical profession would be doing a great thing for the youth and welfare of the world.

MR. McCLINTOCK: I distrust figures from a number of different points because of the potential errors. I think Dr. Williams asked what figures we had of risk and various speakers have emphasized this. Dr. Blonstein replied referring to certain injuries in 6000 bouts. Is he sure that these are all the injuries? There seems to me to be a disincentive to boxers and their trainers to report injuries. What happens if the injury is a somewhat indefinite one and the lad not referred to hospital? Is this put in the records? What proportion of bouts are held outside medical supervision on the professional and amateur boxing side? One of the speakers yesterday referred to quite a lot of contests where there was no medical supervision at all. What training is there of medical officers who officiate at boxing competitions? Please do not think that this is an attack on the concept of medical control in boxing—I am all in favour of some form of medical supervision in sport and industry.

DR. BLONSTEIN: As regards the A.B.A. record of injuries, these injuries are recorded on the boxer's medical card. It is possible that a fracture may not be diagnosed for several days. The reason we can be accurate is because we carry a free insurance scheme for all amateur boxers. If an amateur boxer receives an injury and stays away from work, we pay him a fixed amount each week until he has recovered. Probably over 90 per cent of the injuries are reported as a result of this insurance scheme. As far as outside boxing contests are concerned, I believe there are some private amateur shows that take place, but I cannot give you any definite information. Perhaps Mr. Lovatt can give you some more information on that.

As far as training of medical officers in the A.B.A. is concerned, each medical officer when he joins is given a book of instructions indicating what to look for when he is examining the amateur boxers and telling him how to treat minor injuries and what to do with seriously injured boxers. In addition we have meetings from time to time when these matters are discussed.

COLONEL GRAHAM: There are no professional bouts outside medical supervision in professional boxing. Every tournament has a medical attendant to be at the ringside and observe what is going on in the ring. He must be available to examine every boxer after the contest. With regard to the training of medical officers, we issue a very comprehensive booklet. They are told to look for snags that are not immediately apparent. We tell medical officers to look out for skin diseases which might not easily be thought of and to look out for old cuts and give them much other information.

Obviously it is not practicable to bring them to London for courses as we just have not the funds available to do so.

MR. McDOUGALL: I rise to clear the air regarding this letter which Mr. Doggart quoted from the *British Medical Journal*. There is no boxing bout in Scotland held without a medical officer being present. The letter Mr. Doggart quoted was actually written by the medical

officer who had volunteered for a fee to sit in at the bouts he criti-
cized. We do know that there was some upset between the doctor
concerned and the firm whose sporting interests he looked after.
I think we can disregard the letter. At every bout at which that
doctor was present, the Scottish A.B.A. were there running the show
and providing proper medical cover. When the championships were
held in Glasgow I organized the medical facilities and sat at the
ringside for every bout.

SESSION VI

PANEL DISCUSSION

Chairman

SIR ARTHUR PORRITT, Bt., K.C.M.G., K.C.V.O., C.B.E., F.R.C.S.
Chairman, British Association of Sport and Medicine

Members: RT. HON. BARONESS SUMMERSKILL OF KEN WOOD, P.C.,
M.R.C.S., L.R.C.P.

MR. A. DICKSON WRIGHT, M.S., F.R.C.S., D.T.M. & H.
Surgeon, St. Mary's Hospital and Prince of Wales Hospital

DR. PHILIP KAPLIN, M.B., B.S., M.R.C.S., L.R.C.P.
Member, Medical Sub-Committee, British Boxing Board of
Control

DR. J. A. WAYCOTT, M.B., B.Chir., M.R.C.P., J.P., of
the Middle Temple, Barrister-at-Law
H.M. Deputy Coroner, Borough of Guildford
Medical Officer, Charterhouse School

DR. W. LINDESAY NEUSTATTER, M.D., B.Sc., M.R.C.P.
Physician in Psychiatry, Royal Northern Hospital, etc.
Consultant Psychiatrist, Horton Hospital
Psychiatric Adviser, L.C.C. Schools Health Service

14

PANEL DISCUSSION

QUESTION 1. *Should boxing be rationalized by omitting the head from the target area and allowing hits below the belt on the abdominal muscles?*

MR. DICKSON WRIGHT: I think it is an unthinkable thing to do. It would make an end of boxing. All kinds of armour would be worn to defeat the object of it, and take out all its interest. It would be like having cricket without googlies. Guarding your chin and your face is where the most skill comes in—the best form of defence is attack.

DR. KAPLIN: This is another form of saying that we should have head-guards, and then, I expect, pantaloons and go back to the days when we were like gladiators, wearing armour. Is not this absolutely ludicrous? These people who think that head-guards are the real answer to avoid hurt are wrong—there is a case on record where a professional boxer was actually killed whilst wearing a head-guard. We are losing sight of the noble art of self-defence. This is an art or science—there is no slogging. I cannot see anything more ludicrous than to expect boxers to be allowed to hit below the belt—wherever that is.

LADY SUMMERSKILL: This would be an excellent first step because it would protect the most vulnerable part of the body, the human brain. Of course I agree with the last speaker that he would not like it and boxing would soon end. There would be no chance of a knock-out, no waiting for the moment when you see a man drop and the suspense—will he get up and start again or will he be carried out? Once all that is taken out of boxing there will be no money in it.

(The Chairman remarked that you can have a knockout apart from a blow on the head.)

DR. WAYCOTT: If one removed the head as part of the target this would be a first step. I think the whole thing is so impracticable that we should not waste any further time talking about it.

DR. NEUSTATTER: It might save a head, but what about the future of the human race? (*Laughter.*)

QUESTION 2. *What is the opinion of the panel on the suggestion that as soon as an injury occurs in a boxing match, the fight should be stopped and the verdict awarded to the boxer who is ahead on points?*

DR. KAPLIN: What do you mean by injury? Are you going to stop a contest simply because a boxer is bleeding from one nostril and says, "I am hurt"—I should want a little more definition. An experienced referee would stop the fight immediately if it was necessary—it would depend upon the injury. It is a question of definition.

MR. DICKSON WRIGHT: Whether bouts should be stopped by the referee on account of injury should be left to his discretion, and this has been used very wisely in my experience.

LADY SUMMERSKILL: We have been advised at this conference by the experts that immediately there is a cut that is bleeding, then the contest should be stopped. We have been advised that if a man is knocked out he should be removed to hospital forthwith. That the man in the corner should not be allowed to give first aid—it is not in the interest of the boxer that he should do this, otherwise the cut may not heal.

DR. KAPLIN: We must define injury for a start—you cannot expect anybody who has seen literally thousands and thousands of contests to fall into a trap of this nature to stop boxing.

LADY SUMMERSKILL: That is what the experts told us in the last few days and nobody refuted it.

(The Chairman made some remarks about stopping a fight because of minor injury and the method of awarding points in such a case.)

DR. KAPLIN: . . . This question is so much to the fore . . . if boxer A is at least three-quarters of a point in front at the end of the fourth round and somehow or other by the misuse of the head he gets a cut above the eyebrow and the miscreant is awarded the contest—that is unfair. What referees should do today is to disqualify the miscreant and not allow the chap who is ahead on points to be given a wrong verdict.

MR. DICKSON WRIGHT: That is if injury comes from a foul blow. Injury may come from fair boxing—a man doing very well may then lose a fight because he has got an accidental cut. The contest should be given to the man who is leading on points.

AUDIENCE: I am not going to disagree with Lady Summerskill—we have considered this question in amateur boxing and whilst there is some merit in this suggestion it is not practicable. Quite a lot of amateur boxing is competitive boxing when you go on to the next stage, and if you awarded the verdict to the boy with the cut eye he could not go on to the next stage if he retired. This is one of the hazards and it is accepted that they retire.

QUESTION 3. *Of all the aspects of boxing, which do you most deplore?*

LADY SUMMERSKILL: If you had asked me that question twenty years ago I would have said the injuries which the individual boxers suffered and the hazards involved. Today I must combine it with the spectacle—there is a television set which brings to the people of the household a spectacle every week of men fighting each other and a commentary giving a graphic description of what is happening. Now he has a cut eye, now he is nearly down, and so on. I must say that in my opinion this is debasing. I would remind you that cock-fighting was not made illegal because of the injuries which the cocks suffered, but because of the injuries which the spectators suffered in watching these debasing spectacles—our prisons today are packed with three young men to a cell—they are full of men charged with violent crimes. We are setting up a committee to look into juvenile delinquency. A boy who is not very bright watching these pictures which glamorize violence is encouraged to think that this kind of behaviour is something to be respected and if possible emulated. In this day and age the worst thing is for the spectacles we have had described to us to be seen by unintelligent youths throughout the country. Remember I am talking of members of a captive audience in their little homes, and I believe that we as responsible citizens should recognize that this is a danger to our way of life.

DR. KAPLIN: We are not arbiters of public morals—those are not our affair at present. Nobody has ever seen an advertisement in a newspaper for a professional boxer and you never see any lures to get young men to box. We are dealing today with the medical aspects of boxing. You know as well as I do, those who have had long experience in medicine, that as long as a government allows professional boxing we must control it and, having regard to the fact that we have controlling bodies in professional boxing, moral aspects should remain outside our discussion. I know that occasionally even the Boxing Board of Control falls down, but provided there is professional boxing allowed in this country, so long is it absolutely essential to have control. We have that control and if occasionally something slips through the net it is unfortunate for boxing in this country stands or falls by its medical aspects.

(The Chairman reminded the panel of the question.)

DR. WAYCOTT: The chief objection to the sport is that it is the only sport in which the rules are designed in such a way that the infliction of injury is a deliberate and necessary part of the game. There are sports more dangerous, but injury when it occurs is an accident and the crowd is duly sympathetic. When injury occurs in boxing, it is because it is the intention of the fighter to render his opponent unconscious by a blow to the head. If that is not deliberate infliction of injury, what is?

(The Chairman remarked that it is true that the most dramatic way of winning a contest is to knock your opponent out, but that boxers can be trained to win on points.)

DR. KAPLIN: Many years ago what better sight used there to be than to see young boys and hear the rhythmic pattering of their feet on the floor of the ring. It is not so in these days.

(The Chairman asked what he most deplored in boxing.)

I only deplore the fact that if there is an error in control—that is wrong. No boxer should be put in a position where there is a possibility of him receiving an injury which might prove fatal in any shape or form. Therefore I am so determined that control is absolute in all its shapes, forms and guises. My main concern is that where I see everything should be done where the health or life of a boxer is concerned, so that when he honourably hangs up his gloves, he is still in a position to be a decent member of society and to resume a profession.

MR. DICKSON WRIGHT: In answer to Lady Summerskill, I think that the violence in this country is due to violence in Westerns and crime films and not due to watching boxing. If Lady Summerskill used her powers in the right direction she would stop this sort of violence.

I assure you with all my heart that the prisons are not full of people who watch boxing.

DR. NEUSTATTER: I do not think I can answer the question but I do think Lady Summerskill has raised a very interesting point, although I would not agree with her. I would agree with Mr. Dickson Wright there is a good deal of danger in the televising of the unpleasant forms of criminal violence, but I do not think seeing people box has this effect. There is a natural aggression in all boys, and it is better that this finds expression in watching somebody else, and so I would not agree with her on that particular point.

LADY SUMMERSKILL: Pictures of violence will encourage these things, and if we bring violence to the screen we are making a contribution to these violent displays and to violent and unsociable behaviour.

DR. NEUSTATTER: This is a different type of violence. Boxing is controlled and is rather different from somebody running amok with a gun.

LADY SUMMERSKILL: Why do we have the running commentary? Why is it that when there are two heavyweights slogging it out it is then that the crowd rises up and roars. When there are two lightweight men there is no sound. Randolph Turpin in his last fight in Harringay [cries of "White City" from audience] put up a skilful fight but said when he was leaving "you don't want boxing, you want murder. It is violence you want to see."

DR. NEUSTATTER: There might be a certain amount of truth in this, but I would not agree that it is so for most households. Watching boxing does not have this bad effect. I agree that the heavyweights slogging are more sensational but it does not make me want to go out and hit people.

DR. KAPLIN: Flyweights and bantamweights may fight in absolute silence, but after each round the skill has produced such applause that you could not hear. It does not apply only to slogging.

(MR. J. SOLOMONS (audience) pointed out that Randolph Turpin's last fight was at the White City and he had heard Lady Summerskill put this argument before.)

DR. WILLIAMS (audience): There is one matter in which I would like to support Lady Summerskill. I deplore very much the sadistic reporting and commentating on fights, but I do not see that you can condemn boxing for the way in which it is described and reported. It has no effect on the nature of the thing itself. You may like the way a particular columnist or a particular newspaper reports or you may dislike it, but you cannot condemn boxing because it is written up in certain papers as a glorified blood-bath, nor can you praise it just because it is written up as a lyrical demonstration of art.

MAJOR WEBB (*audience*): Lady Summerskill described boxers as being young thugs or similar wording. I returned last night from the team championships of the Junior Soldiers Wing—both teams got together and they were the greatest of friends. Boxing in the Army does a great deal of good and stimulates friendships.

MR. RIDLER (*audience*): I have a great respect for what Lady Summerskill says because what she is saying she means for the benefit of the boys. But surely her answer indicated that it was the reactions of the people who were watching which she deplored so much more. But nobody who boxes can control the people who watch them. Thousands of boys take part in this sport. I have taken part in boxing from the age of 11 and I am capable of holding arguments and am physically fit for my age. These people who suffer are unfortunate—it is just one of those things. But to deprive these boys who want to box because of the small minority who are injured or because of crowd reaction seems to me to be going too far.

LADY SUMMERSKILL: But unless you have spectators you will not have a boxing match organized. None of these people would be able to go on if there was no money available from paying audiences [cries of "nonsense!"]. You tell me that the spectator really plays such a small part—this is absolutely news to me.

AUDIENCE: I have one comment on what Lady Summerskill says —we ought to distinguish between actions in the heat of the moment and actions which are going to be carried on in after life. When a crowd starts fighting at a football match this does not mean that they are going to be thugs for ever more. It is what happens continually in life . . . I am not particularly interested in boxing although I would not ban it. The thing I do admire most is the behaviour in schools' boxing where the audience is taught to control their feelings until the end of the round and then applaud. I wish this was extended throughout boxing generally.

LADY SUMMERSKILL: The whole point about a football match is

to score a goal—the point about boxing is to render your opponent insensible. The two things have a different appeal to the emotions of the human being.

(The Chairman remarked that the contest is usually won on points—by far the majority are not won by knockouts.)

LADY SUMMERSKILL: When these men go into the ring they hope for a knockout. We have already heard of how many amateurs were knocked out—the amateur may wear a little vest but he is knocked out just as much as the professional.

DR. KAPLIN: Less than one in fifty fights end in knockouts. It is absolutely wrong to spread this sort of statement.

LADY SUMMERSKILL: It is often his primary objective to knock his opponent out.

QUESTION 4. *The Panel is asked to comment on the effectiveness of protective clothing for the head—should the authorities concerned make the wearing of headgear compulsory?*

DR. WAYCOTT: Yes, certainly, for all. The reason why I regard it as important is that the head is the most vulnerable part of the body in boxing. Although a head-guard (as we have heard) cannot give total protection any more than a crash helmet, at least it can give some protection, and this is very much in the minds of the American Forces who require their people to wear head-guards. It is used by a number of different organizations in various parts of the world, and I think that this is something that ought to come in in this country. It should be made as safe as possible, and this view must be shared by a great number of people in the world. We saw today a pneumatic headgear which was of great interest to us. This is an advance which ought to be considered very carefully. This particular design is wrong—it does not protect the chin from the punch that causes the swirling of the brain which is the cause of some cerebral damage—this form of head-guard is defective in that way. The sooner the medical objections to the sport and the degree of control of the sport will come more into line with enlightened medical opinion the better for all.

DR. KAPLIN: The only thing I feel is most important is to make absolutely sure that when a boxer does get a punch on the chin his head should not hit the canvas of the floor with such a thud because this is the primary cause of sub- or extra-dural haemorrhages. These theories of a countout or a knockout are still in dispute: whether it is due to dislocation of the brain or a clash of the brain stem against the tentorium, to reflex or to nervous connections in the carotid sinus, I do not know. Going back to the head, the cerebro-spinal fluid is sufficient to counteract these swirling movements provided you do not hit your head on the floor of the ring. In nine cases out of ten, the boxer will go down for a count of 5, or 6 or 7. I am 100 per cent in favour that no boxing area should be registered or allowed to promote contests without a proper floor matting. As for your head-guards, it would look ludicrous, and it is not 100 per cent safe. I can produce a record of a boxer killed in the ring wearing head-guards. Secondly, I agree with Dr. Waycott about protecting the chin. The boxer ought to wear a sort of triangular bandage.

DR. WAYCOTT: Dr. Kaplin feels that the floor is the most important thing.

DR. KAPLIN: There is no record of a man being killed where appropriate floor matting is used.

MR. DICKSON WRIGHT: A head-guard only saves you from a thick ear. It does not really safeguard you from anything else but cosmetic damage and I am against it.

AUDIENCE: In the contest between Spinks and O'Neill held several years ago at Wembley there was one of those protected floors but O'Neill went off to the hospital and nearly died.

DR. KAPLIN: The injury which O'Neill suffered was told to me. I immediately rang the surgeon regarding the extent of the injury and the type of pathology that was found. I do not know whether there was any floor matting.

AUDIENCE: At the time of the Spinks–O'Neill fight this type of protective floor matting was not in use—it was of a different kind.

AUDIENCE: The most important point is to prevent a maxillo-facial injury by a properly constructed made-to-measure mouth shield. It would be ideal if the young boys could get this shield under the National Health Service. It costs less than any fractured tooth.

QUESTION 5. *Is it true that the vast majority of amateur boxers come from the same socio-economic group? If so, why?*

LADY SUMMERSKILL: We have heard so much about amateur boxers. I have observed that those who have spoken about them have stressed "I am talking about amateur boxers". It is the simple, ignorant boy who boxes. The headmaster of Bradfield (who will soon become headmaster of Eton) has forbidden boxing there. They have no boxing at Gordonstoun. We have the medical officer of Charterhouse, where they do not box, here. In the paper this week Oxford University was finding it difficult to find a team. These places are well advised by first-class medical officers. If it is considered unfit for these boys to learn boxing why should the boys in Camberwell learn it today? Is it only one class? It begins to look as though it is.

MR. DICKSON WRIGHT: Charterhouse does not play rugger. There is enough public-school boxing to have contests every year.

MR. LOVATT (*audience*): Unfortunately public-school boxing is not carried on to the extent that we would like it. Certain headmasters have views similar to Lady Summerskill. The bulk of schools receive no control. We have tried to get into the public schools. It may be that you have something and there is a little snobbish feeling about boxing. We have people of all classes and conditions. We may have the majority from the poorer classes but I can assure you we are well represented from all sections of society.

AUDIENCE: Mention has been made of the headmaster of Bradfield who has stopped boxing at that school. It is quite plain that the particular medical officer for Bradfield objected to boxing. He was probably a very satisfactory medical officer in other respects. The headmaster was particularly careful not to commit himself on what he would do when he was at Eton. His particular doctor disliked it and he thought fit to stop it. And therefore we cannot draw any conclusions from this case.

DR. NEUSTATTER: On the socio-economic aspect of the thing: Lady Summerskill mentioned juvenile delinquency in relation to boxing. One of the essential causes is that in overcrowded districts there is a gross lack of recreational facilities and boxing is a recreation which can be comparatively easily obtained, unlike cricket where you need a large field and a whole day to occupy only twenty-two men. Lady Summerskill is, of course, entitled to her views that boxing is not a good thing, but from what I have heard I am not convinced that it does more harm than good in that these boys get recreation instead of going around on the streets. I did not hear sufficiently convincing evidence to outweigh the good it does. If you weigh one against the other, it makes me feel I would come down on the side of boxing.

LADY SUMMERSKILL: I absolutely agree about the streets but surely there are other sports these boys could indulge in, not only boxing.

DR. NEUSTATTER: I agree that boxing is not the only sport, but it is a very difficult thing to find the necessary space for others.

MR. DICKSON WRIGHT: Boys' clubs would be lost without their boxing.

MR. HAMILTON (*audience*): Lady Summerskill might be interested to know that one boxing promoter said he would prefer public schoolboys because they were less easily put off.

LADY SUMMERSKILL: Public schoolboys are too wise.

MR. SOLOMONS (*audience*): I would like to ask Lady Summerskill this question as she does not like school boxing. I asked her this question about ten years ago. Has her son done any boxing when he was at school?

LADY SUMMERSKILL: Perhaps he did do some boxing at St. Paul's. I do not know.

MR. SOLOMONS (*audience*): I pointed out to you how good he was (*laughter*).

MAJOR WEBB (*audience*): Sandhurst box regularly and I think they may be said to be in the upper class. Boxing there has a wide range. Many officers, N.C.O.s and soldiers box. There are headmasters and commanding officers of units who dislike boxing and they condemn it out of hand. Many of the people under them would like to box but because of the ban they have no opportunity to do so. We must respect their views even though they are the views of minorities.

DR. WAYCOTT: As far as Cranwell is concerned we have young men who are taught to land jet aeroplanes at high speeds when the utmost skill, co-ordination and balance is required. The Commandant of R.A.F. Cranwell, because he has been worried about impairment of co-ordination resulting from boxing injuries, has banned boxing.

AUDIENCE: Surely individuals, except schoolboys in certain circumstances, are fully aware of the danger of injury. If they are aware of the danger, it is their own life and they can do what they like with it.

LADY SUMMERSKILL: That is rather unkind. We are adults and this must mean that we must protect the young. The youngster cannot really judge for himself.

AUDIENCE: I did stress that I was not really referring to school-boys. A fully grown man is quite capable of deciding what he wants to do with his life.

LADY SUMMERSKILL: About the punch-drunk syndrome?

DR. BLONSTEIN: Dr. Waycott mentioned Cranwell. My son was a medical officer at Cranwell. Pilots not allowed to box were allowed to play rugby football and every weekend they had at least four fractured noses in pilots as a result of rugby.

LADY SUMMERSKILL: Boxing is more dangerous than rugby. The R.A.F. refused to let them box because of the danger.

DR. WAYCOTT: You do not fly an aeroplane with your nose but with your brain.

QUESTION 6. *Protagonists of boxing claim that boxing is a safe sport because in absolute terms there are fewer injuries. Is it not dishonest to employ absolute figures instead of relative figures, which give a more accurate and honest comparison?*

MR. DICKSON WRIGHT: I think this is a fair question. It is almost impossible of achievement, and to compile statistics on these relative scores would be very difficult. Statistics are not only a matter of numbers but in the amount of sport indulged in. What we do know is that every sport has a risk and we should not give up sports because of risk. In rugby there are many injuries such as spinal injuries which are severe but do not stop people playing. I agree we should consider relative risk, but you would find it jolly hard to do so.

LADY SUMMERSKILL: Over the past two days, time after time we have been told about the number of accidents in cricket, rugby and other sports and by comparison how small they are in boxing. I am told that in this country there are only 400 registered boxers and not 4000 as before—this is a terrific decline. To compare the accident rate of these with the hundreds of thousands playing football this afternoon is quite unreasonable and dishonest.

CHAIRMAN: I try to remain impartial, but in my opinion this is a tiny problem altogether and we want to keep that in perspective. It really is not of great importance compared to numerous other things which do produce serious injuries.

LADY SUMMERSKILL: We have to realize we are not talking about obvious injuries only, but also syndromes such as punch-drunken-ness where the initial signs cannot be detected and when they are detected they cannot be cured and the condition may be permanent.

Let us consider these conditions on one side. We accept that they may be fairly small in number but the condition that the young man suffers from forty or fifty fights very few people can diagnose. We have heard statistics, but the young man whose wife finds him difficult is more than a mere statistical figure. Suppose such a man who has had about fifty fights goes to his busy G.P., no details are written on his record card. The Ministry of Health cannot be bothered to follow these up because it is not their job to pick out those that might be related to young men fighting. These statistics are completely fallacious.

DR. KAPLIN: The first important point is to discuss this question of punch-drunkenness. The early signs of punch-drunkenness cannot be evaluated or diagnosed in a consulting room or the out-patient department of a clinic at a national hospital or any other clinical or laboratory method. The early signs of this can only be diagnosed at the ringside, and those who do not go boxing can have no possible idea of what may occur in the early stages. If a medical officer goes boxing regularly he will suddenly see a boxer showing evidence of certain manifestations. He is no longer alert, his timing is bad, his footwork is bad, he develops a high coefficient of absorption for punishment. These are the signs of the early punch-drunk syndrome. If at that stage his licence is taken away he will not have persistent symptoms. I have taken boxers' licences away for fifteen years and more for these specific signs and I am proud to say that none of them developed punch-drunkenness. It is, of course, difficult to make an exact prognosis. At the risk of repeating myself, I wish to say you must know what you are talking about when you say that statistics are fallacious and talk a lot of spurious sophistry on these points. Serious injuries are always recorded and a history taken of everything significant, especially when a contest has been stopped. Every professional boxer has a complete record of his boxing history recorded at head office. Chronic brain injury may occur here and there, but it must be very rare. It was on my instigation that a very famous boxer was stopped from boxing because I saw these signs at the ringside. This man is not going to box any more; he has had a series of hard-fought contests. He appealed and he called Dr. McDonald Critchley to give evidence for him, but his appeal has not been allowed.

MR. SOLOMONS (*audience*): Freddy Mills has had about 300 fights and is now a very popular entertainer. Several other boxers—Henry

Armstrong, Gene Tunney, Jack Dempsey—have done very well.

DR. ROBSON (*audience*): The original question related to the necessity for accurate statistical information about injury rate based on the number of contestants and number of hours in which the sport is practised. May I take this opportunity of appealing to anybody who has any valid statistics either to make them public or try and pool these statistics so that we can get accurate statistical information and can accurately compare one sport with another and make an attempt to know in the future what we are talking about.

AUDIENCE: These statistics are available in insurance companies. The percentage accident rate is about half that for football. That discounts any question of numbers. The rate to cover boxers is much lower than for footballers.

QUESTION 7. *Why does the governing body of professional boxing not permit the medical officer greater control, including allowing him to stop the fight if he thinks this necessary on medical grounds?*

DR. KAPLIN: Every referee, from the moment he is given an area, is given a grounding on the medical aspects. The referee is the final arbiter in the ring, and rightly so. No medical officer should be put in the position of making a diagnosis during a fight. If there was a trickle of blood, can you possibly imagine what would happen in the hall if the medical officer said: "You have a fractured septum", and stopped the fight? Let the referee do it, that is what he is there for.

QUESTION 8. *When an amateur boxer turns professional no notice is taken of his past record. Should there not be liaison in this matter?*

DR. KAPLIN: The British Boxing Board of Control today have a very happy liaison with the Amateur Boxing Association. When a certain boxer turned professional it came to my knowledge behind the scenes that he had been in a mental hospital, because one of his colleagues wrote me a letter. We will continue to have the greatest liaison between amateur bodies and ourselves.

QUESTION 9. *Can boxing or boxing training have any benefit for other sports?*

DR. WAYCOTT: Boxing means a rigorous training for co-ordination and balance. These things can be turned to good account in other sports.

QUESTION 10. *Should boxing be banned for medical reasons?*

LADY SUMMERSKILL: Sitting here listening and looking I felt that many of you here must have been a little bewildered at hearing doctors not speaking with one voice. I think that it is right to say that this conference has reflected the views of people all over the world, especially what the northern European countries are feeling. In Denmark the Public Health Board is in favour of prohibition. In Belgium they have so strengthened controls that boxing will go. Little Iceland has prohibited it. The Scandinavian countries are respected all over the world and in Norway the Chief Medical Officer is so important that the United Nations use him and he wants it prohibited. In the United States, New York State has just had a big inquiry. This is not just an *ad hoc* conference because we feel that our views have been expressed in all these countries by people who have similar attitudes. We are only a small part of a very big chain in opinion.

DR. KAPLIN: I should hate to go away from here, as an old opponent of Lady Summerskill's, feeling that there was any personal animosity. We differ on one fundamental basis. Should boxing be stopped for any possible reason? If the answer is no, it must be perfectly controlled.

DR. NEUSTATTER: You may dislike boxing because of the alleged aggression or because of the physical dangers, but there are dangers in every sport. I am not satisfied that boxing has many more than any other sport.

DR. WAYCOTT: I should like to see greater control both in amateur and professional boxing. It seems to me that one of the ways in which this can be done is to improve measures of protection. For those who wish to see the sport banned, I can see no hope that their wishes will be realized in the immediate future. The sport can be made less dangerous and one of the ways is the development of the appropriate headgear. The same situation arose in duelling, where to bear a scar was a mark of honour; this was prohibited by law and duelling has been transformed into fencing and fencing is one of the most elegant and skilful sports which you may ever hope to see. This sort of protection can be made available to boxers. Boxing can be made safer by strict medical control and appropriate head-guards.

If you go away thinking of nothing else but this point, the conference will have been very worth while indeed and I would certainly commend to all of you that you do so.

DR. KAPLIN: I agree that we need every possible safeguard in boxing.

Lady Summerskill thanked the chairman for presiding in such an impartial way and SIR ARTHUR PORRITT concluded with the following remarks:

By and large the problem divided itself up into:

(a)   Amateur and professional boxing.

(b)   Protection as against abolition.

(c)   Amity and friendship between all concerned for those who want to do the best for sport in this country.

This is really our aim and our object.

EPILOGUE

DURING and after the conclusion of the conference, considerable private discussion took place amongst the speakers and members of the audience in addition to the sessions of discussion that formed part of the formal proceedings. From such discussion as well as from the papers presented, a number of salient areas of general agreement seemed to be emerging. Although not in any way part of the formal proceedings these areas of agreement would seem to be worthy of record.

Firstly, then, it was generally agreed that boxing did carry a definite risk, both of death and of disability. Insufficient information was available to determine the degree of risk in statistical terms, and without that information and thus knowledge of the degree of risk, it was impossible objectively to determine whether or not the risk was acceptable. As the chairman of the first session pointed out, "if we are not going to cease to live as human beings we must accept a certain measure of calculated risk". Until, therefore, the degree of risk is formally calculated, its acceptance or otherwise must be based solely on subjective criteria.

It was very apparent that many of the speakers were not entirely objective in their approach to the problems under discussion. This, of course, was understandable. However, partisanship was in a few cases perhaps carried rather far. Thus, it was quite notable that where figures were quoted they tended to be quoted in absolute rather than relative terms. A comparison of injury rates in different sports, for example, can only be valid when the units of expression are the same, such as "per man involved" or better "per man hour". It is true that the number of deaths due to boxing is lower than the number due to cricket. Presentation of absolute figures can only obscure the fundamental issues at stake.

Secondly, it was apparent that discussion and consideration of medical aspects of boxing should be broken down according to the types of boxing, amateur and professional, and that amateur boxing should be further subdivided according to whether or not it was

practised under the direct control of the Amateur Boxing Association
and the Schools and Services Amateur Boxing Associations.

Most people did feel that the authorities controlling amateur
boxing, where they could exert a direct influence, were aware of the
risks and were genuinely attempting to minimize them. Where amateur
boxing was practised away from direct control, for example in some
schools, unnecessary risks were taken. The plea of the secretary of
the Schools A.B.A. for all schoolboy boxing to be brought under the
jurisdiction of that body was therefore received with some sympathy.

Professional boxing, on the other hand, was more readily criti-
cized. It seemed to be generally felt that although the medical sub-
committee of the British Boxing Board of Control was doing its best,
the whole structure of the sport was such that financial considerations
were of too great an importance. Thus the impression that too many
fights were permitted to continue beyond what was medically reasonable could not entirely be dispersed by the protagonists of professional boxing, nor did the reasons brought forward for giving the
referee, as third party, sole discretion as to whether or not to stop a
fight on medical grounds find universal acceptance. It was particularly interesting that none of the subsequent speakers nor any member of the audience connected with professional boxing made any
reply to the comment of Mr. B. N. Bailey that a fight should be
stopped immediately a cut appeared above the eye.

What emerged most clearly from the conference is that too little is
known of the medical sequels of boxing and of their rate of occurrence and significance for conclusions yet to be drawn with any degree
of real objectivity. If one had to indicate the general reaction to
boxing as a whole from the medical point of view as it appeared to
emerge from this conference, one would probably be fair in saying
that boxing gained a narrow points verdict on a split decision.